Welcome to the 3rd local edition of Let's G-
working to help Great Ormond Street Ho
Researched by Sabine N

Through the sale of these guides we aimed to raise £3500 in 1998 an(
towards a mobile x-ray unit for use in performing chest x-rays on child
children are too sick to be moved to the Radiology Department for the
We are proud to announce that a 5 pence donation to the above char.
Children" book sold in the 1999 season. Thank you for your support.

Registered Charity No. 235825 © G(_. ...

CONTENTS

B2	Map References - refer to map on page 2 and locate the grid square to help you find out where everything is.	EH	English Heritage Property
		NT	National Trust Property
Ⓐ	Price code (defined in key on most pages) to help you budget your visits.	Q♦	Birthday parties are organised where you see these signs.
Schools	School party facilities here.	*Open all year*	Winter opening too!

A telephone number is given for most entries. Should you require special facilities for someone with a
disability, please call before your visit to check suitability.

Cube Publications, Bank House, Mavins Road, Farnham, Surrey GU9 8JS
Phone/Fax 01252 722761 or 01425 615648
ISBN 1 871808 83 9

Ordnance Survey

MAP

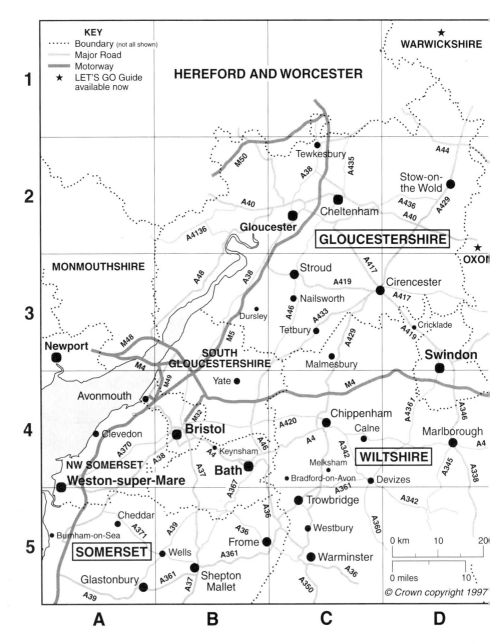

Where's the best place to go for

HUMONGOUS FUN, WICKED THRILLS?

and a great day out with the **KIDS?**

Thorpe Park

It's got to be The GreatThorpe Park

FOR the most humongous day out, get down to The Great Thorpe Park where you can now get a great deal more for a great deal less with my funtastical Harley Pass Season Ticket. It gives you the whole The Great Thorpe Park to enjoy as often as you like and is valid for a whole year from date of purchase. You can pick up an application form or call our hotline now and we'll rush one to you. **01932 562633**.

The greatest days out are at The Great Thorpe Pa

BOAT TRIPS & TRAIN TRIPS

Have a change from the car. Try a train or a boat trip.

BOAT TRIPS

A4

from Clevedon. Travel by paddle steamer to Bristol. *Sailings from May to Oct.* 01446 720656.

Ⓖ **from Weston-super-Mare** Knightstone Causeway. Day trips run to Steep Holm Island which is a nature reserve. (See "Wildlife" chapter.) 01934 632307.

B3

from Sharpness. Two hour cruises down River Severn to Clevedon (note these are not round trips). Longer cruises down Severn Estuary along Exmoor coast to Lynton and Lynmouth. Limited sailings during the Summer. 01446 720656.

B4

Ⓒ **from Bath** Pulteney Bridge. **The Bath Boating Station,** a unique boating facility, is located upstream of Pulteney Bridge on the River Avon. It has the only fleet of punts in the West Country and also the largest fleet of Thames Rowing Skiffs in England. All of these boats are period pieces and provide a most pleasant way of exploring this beautiful stretch of river. Tuition in the art of poling a punt is available from the boating station staff. For those who wish to receive a conducted tour of the river, motorised trips are available. *Open daily, 10.30am-6pm, April-end Oct.* Telephone for Winter opening times. 01225 466407. (See Advert page 6.)

from Bristol City Docks, daily trips around the city docks calling at SS Great Britain every 20 minutes. Round trip about 40 minutes. Longer trips to Bristol Bridge at weekends and school holidays from Apr-Sept. 0117 9273416.

Schools Floating Harbour. Trips on 1920s river steamer or historic narrowboat to Conham, Hanham, Saltford Lock or up the Avon Gorge under the Suspension Bridge to the Bristol Channel. Also available, tours of the city docks with commentary. *Cruises run from Easter to Sept daily.* 0117 9268157.

Also sail up the River Severn or the Avon, or along the Somerset coast in Summer. 01446 720656.

Industrial Museum. Occasional trips on historic steam tug from just outside the museum (see Industrial Museum in "Historic Sites" chapter).

C2

Ⓓ **from Tewkesbury** Riverside Walk. One hour trips in all weather waterbus. Cruises in Summer months only. 01684 275906.

Ⓓ **from Gloucester** National Waterways Museum, (see also "Historic Sites" **Schools** chapter). Trips on Queen Bodicea II, one of the little boats from the Dunkirk flotilla. Forty-five minute round canal trip or 3 hour trip up River Severn. Also occasional sailings to Tewkesbury or Sharpness. *Operate Mar-end Oct.* 01452 318054.

C4

from Bradford-on-Avon. Public and charter trips along the Kennet & Avon Canal, *Easter-end Sept.* Board at the Wharf. 01380 721279.

from Devizes The Wharf. Locally built narrow boats on the Kennet & Avon Canal. *Easter-end Sept.* 01380 728504.

TRAIN TRIPS

B2

Ⓑ **Perrygrove Railway,** near Coleford, on the B4228. Enjoy a trip on the 15" NG **Schools** steam railway, while the children solve clues to the woodland treasure hunt and claim their reward in the indoor village. Picnic area and cafe. *Open every Sun from Apr-end Oct.* Telephone for other dates and opening times. 01594 834991.

B3

Ⓓ / Ⓔ **Dean Forest Railway,** Lydney. The round trip takes between 30 and 40 **Schools** minutes. *The railway is open every Sun and Bank Hol Mon from Apr-end Sept and every Wed from Jun-beg Sept and selected dates in Dec.* 01594 843423 or 01594 845840.

5

B4
Open all year
🔍

Avon Valley Railway, Bitton. Take a forty five minute journey on a steam train along the scenic Avon Valley. Special events throughout the year including "Friends of Thomas" and Santa specials. See the trains being lovingly restored and find out about work to extend the line towards Bath. Visit the station buffet and watch the trains steaming by. *Open every weekend throughout the year, trains run from May to Sept at weekends, Bank Hol Mons and for Christmas specials.* 0117 9327296. (See Advert below.)

ⓑ **Industrial Museum,** Bristol, take a short trip on a steam train along the docks from the museum. (See Industrial Museum in "Historic Sites" chapter.)

B5
Schools
Open all year
🔍

ⓒ **East Somerset Railway,** Cranmore, is about three miles from Shepton Mallet, off the A361 to Frome. A round journey on these steam hauled passenger trains takes 32 minutes. There is a Victorian-style engine shed where the workshop can be viewed from a special platform, picnic areas, children's play area, art gallery, museum, gift shop and restaurant. Look out for the special steam days. 01749 880417.

C2

ⓓ **Gloucestershire Warwickshire Railway,** Toddington. 13 mile round trip on part of the former Great Western main line between Stratford-upon-Avon and Cheltenham. *Operates weekends from beg Mar-end Oct, daily in some school holidays. Various special events including "Santa Special" during Dec.* 01242 621405.

C3

ⓒ **National Rail Station,** Kemble. Pretty Cotswold stone station. The diesel train journey to Swindon takes approximately 20 minutes and is a good trip for children who want to experience train travel. Incorporate it with a visit to the Great Western Railway Museum in Swindon. (See "Historic Sites" chapter.) 0345 484950.

D3
ⓑ / ⓒ
Open all year

Swindon & Cricklade Railway, Blunsdon. Trips up the track on 'steaming' days. (See "Historic Sites" chapter.) *Open weekends.* 01793 771615.

FIND THE REAL RIVER AT BATH
The Bath Boating Station
Forester Road, Bathwick, Bath *Telephone 01225-466407*
Open Daily April-September inclusive 10am-6pm

A unique Victorian boating station with tea gardens and restaurant. Traditional wooden skiffs and punts for hire by the hour or day. This is a pleasant way for a family to spend a summer day on the prettiest reach of the river Avon at Bath. There is abundant wildlife, kingfishers, herons, geese etc. The use of punts is a speciality and tuition is available in the art of poling. River trips are available from the Pulteney Bridge at frequent intervals.

FARMS, WILDLIFE AND NATURE PARKS

Flora and fauna at its best for you to enjoy.

MAP REFS | **PRICE CODES**

A4 Ⓓ Schools Open all year 🔍
Sea Life Centre, Marine Parade, **Weston-super-Mare.** Explore the undersea world of the Bristol Channel without getting wet. With a dramatic underwater tunnel and variety of environments, the Centre is full of interest for all ages. Groups by arrangement. *Open Summer daily, 10am-5pm, ring for Winter opening times. Closed 25th Dec.* 01934 641603.

Ⓖ
Steep Holm Island, off **Weston-super-Mare,** covering 50 acres, is located in the Bristol Channel about 5 miles offshore. The island is owned and run by a charity, the Kenneth Allsop Trust, as a wildlife sanctuary. Boat trips can be made to the island Apr-Oct.. (See "Trips" chapter.)

A5 Ⓒ Schools Open all year 🔍
Animal Farm Country Park, Red Rd, **Berrow.** Feed the friendly animals, cuddle the pets and see rare breeds, all set in 25 acres of delightful countryside. There is a huge play area outside and new for 1999, an indoor adventure play arena. Tea room and gift shop. *Open Easter-Sept 10am-5.30pm, Oct-Easter, 10am-4.30pm.* 01278 751628.

Ⓒ Schools 🔍
Badger and Wildlife Centre, Secret World, New Road, **East Huntspill.** Discover wildlife displays, a badger observation sett and different breeds of farm and wildlife animals. Play areas, nature trail, visitor centre and restaurant. *Open daily, Easter-1st Oct, 10am-6pm. Winter months, 10am-5pm, or dusk. Closed Jan.* 01278 783250.

Ⓒ Schools Open all year 🔍
Court Farm, Wolvershill Rd, **Banwell.** Help bottle feed the baby animals and learn about modern and traditional farming methods. There are special activities including owl talks and ferret shows. Play area, indoor adventure fort and tea room. *Open Tues-Sun, 10am-5.30pm and every day during school hols.* 01934 822383.

B2 Ⓑ Schools
Blakemore Farm, **Longhope,** on the A4136 between Little London and Longhope, is home to Britain's largest herd of angora goats and their fleece is used to produce garments. Enjoy a farm walk and feed the animals. Picnic area and refreshments. Groups welcome, by appointment. 01452 830630.

Ⓒ Schools 🔍
National Birds of Prey Centre, **Newent.** Enjoy watching falcons, eagles, vultures, hawks and owls during well-explained flying demonstrations held three or four times a day. Home to over 300 birds of prey, there is also an education centre, and coffee shop. New for 1999 is a large playground and extensive picnic area. *Open 1st Feb-30th Nov, daily, 10.30am-5.30pm (or dusk if earlier).* Under 4s Ⓕ. 01531 820286.

Ⓑ
Puzzle Wood, **Coleford,** 14 acres of woodland and pre-Roman open cast iron ore mine. The paths were laid nearly 200 years ago to form a very unusual maze. Explore wooden bridges, passage ways through the rock and many dead-ends and circles. Picnic area and tea room. *Open daily, Easter-end Oct, 11am-6pm. Closed Mons except Bank Hols.* 01594 833187.

B3 Ⓑ
Butterfly Farm, **Berkeley Castle,** is midway between Bristol and Gloucester, just off the A38. Set in a walled garden, adjacent to the car park of this beautiful Castle (see "Historic Sites" chapter), exotic and British butterflies are farmed, and can be seen in free flight amongst lovely and unusual flowers and plants. *Open Apr-May: Tues-Sun 1-5pm, Jun & Sept: Tues-Sat 11am-5pm, Sun 1-5pm, Jul & Aug: Mon-Sat 11am-5pm, Sun 1-5pm, Oct: Sun only 1-5pm, all Bank Hol Mons, 11am-5pm.* 01453 810332. (See Advert page 40).

Map Ref: Please refer to map on page 2.
Price Codes for a family of four: Ⓐ: less than £5 Ⓑ: £5-£10 Ⓒ: £10-£15 Ⓓ: £15-£20 Ⓔ: £20-£30 Ⓖ:- Over £30 Ⓕ: Free
Schools: Range of educational opportunities available. 🔍 Birthday parties organised.

Ⓓ
Schools
🔍

Cattle Country, Berkeley Heath. There is something for everyone at this farm park. See the exotic cattle including bison, feed the wild boar from an overhead feeding platform or stroll around the farm trail. There is an extensive adventure playground with giant mouse wheel and splash pool. Indoors there is a soft play area with Drop slide, Astra slide and roller racers. Cafe and picnic area. *Open Easter-end Sept, Sat, Sun & School hols, 10.30am-5pm.* 01453 810220.

Ⓒ
Schools
🔍

Oldown, Tockington, near Thornbury. From a quiet stroll through 80 acres of ancient woodland to the Forest Challenge with its fireman's pole out of a tree and tube slide, there is something for all ages on this working farm. Young visitors are sure to enjoy the enclosed woodland play area, feeding the animals and mini tractor driving, while learning is fun in the Farm Education Centre with its live exhibits and hands-on models. There are weekend displays during the Summer, tractor and trailer rides, picnic areas and a Picnic House, together with restaurant, farm shop and market garden. *Open Easter-end Oct, Tues-Sun and Bank Hol Mons, 10am-6pm.* 01454 413605 or ring 07000 Oldown. (See Advert page 10.)

Ⓓ
Schools
Open all year

Wildlife & Wetlands Trust, Slimbridge. Situated on the banks of the River Severn between Bristol and Gloucester, this 800 acre reserve is home to the world's largest collection of exotic wildfowl. Feed the birds, visit the new children's play area, sustainable garden, tropical house and pond zone. Major new developments for 1999 include a lakeside entrance, dramatic new observation tower, enlarged visitor centre, enhanced shop and restaurant. Special events and activities during School hols. *Open daily, 9.30am-5pm (4pm in Winter). Closed 25th Dec.* 01453 890065.

Ⓒ
Schools
🔍

Avon Valley Country Park, Keynsham, covers 32 acres with a vast selection of attractions from animals to assault courses. There is a children's play area, large slide, mini golf and boating and fishing on the river, as well as nature trails along riverside paths. There is also a barbecue and picnic area. *Open 28th Mar-1st Nov, Tues-Sun, Bank Hol Mons and daily in School hols, 10am-6pm.* 0117 9864929.

Ⓔ
Schools
Open all year

Bristol Zoo Gardens, Clifton. Enjoy an exciting real life experience and see over 300 species of wildlife in beautiful gardens. New for Summer 1999 is a seal and penguin exhibit with fantastic underwater viewing, to join favourites such as Gorilla Island, Bug World, Twilight World, Aquarium, Reptile House and children's play area. The popular 'hands-on' Activity Centre, interactive Zoolympics trail, special events and feeding time talks make it an educational as well as enjoyable day out. Each visit will also help fund important conservation work. *Open daily, 9am-approx 5.30pm (4.30pm Winter). Closed 25th Dec.* 0117 9738951. www.bristolzoo.org.uk (See Advert page 10.)

Ⓑ / Ⓒ
Open all year

Prior Park Landscape Garden, NT, Ralph Allen Drive, **Bath.** This lovely garden has a Palladian bridge, fish ponds and fine views. There is no car park and visitors are asked to arrive either by bus, bicycle or on foot. Sturdy shoes are recommended to negotiate the steep paths down into the valley, especially when damp. *Open Wed-Mon, 12-5.30pm or dusk if earlier. Closed 25th-26th Dec and 1st Jan.* 01225 833422. 24 hr Information Line: 0891 335242.

Ⓕ Schools
Open all year

Windmill Hill City Farm, Bedminster, Bristol. See "Free Places" chapter.

Ⓒ
Schools
🔍

Norwood Farm, Bath Road, **Norton St. Philip,** is an immaculate organic working farm with beautiful views across Somerset. Rare breeds of ponies, goats, sheep, cows and film-star pigs to be fed and stroked. Farm walk, picnic and play area and cafeteria. *Open 21st Mar-20th Sept, daily, 10.30am-6pm.* 01373 834356. (See Advert page 20.)

Map Ref: Please refer to map on page 2.
Price Codes for a family of four: Ⓐ: less than £5 Ⓑ: £5-£10 Ⓒ: £10-£15 Ⓓ: £15-£20 Ⓔ: £20-£30 Ⓖ:- Over £30 Ⓕ: Free
Schools: Range of educational opportunities available. 🔍 Birthday parties organised.

8

MAP REFS	PRICE CODES

C2 ⓓ Schools — Open all year

Prinknash Bird Park, near **Cranham,** off the A46. Hand-feed the peacocks and numerous waterfowl in this small park set in the grounds of the Abbey. Walk through the Golden Wood to the Haunted Monks Pool and throw food to the trout. There is also a deer park and a small play area. *Open daily, Summer, 10am-5pm, 4pm in Winter. Closed 25th, 26th Dec, 1st Jan, Good Fri.* 01452 812727.

C3 ⓑ Schools — Open all year

Westonbirt Arboretum, near **Tetbury,** covers 600 acres. See giant Redwoods to delicate acacias and enjoy woodland walks in the ever-changing seasons. Discovery days for children during the school holidays. Visitors' centre and café. *Open daily, 10am-8pm, or dusk if earlier.* 01666 880220.

C4 ⓓ / ⓔ

Bowood House and Gardens, Calne. Set in one of the most beautiful parks in the country, landscaped by 'Capability' Brown with sloping lawns stretching away from the House to the lake beyond, this 100 acre park contains many exotic trees in the arboretum and pinetum, a Cascade Waterfall, Doric Temple and Hermit's Cave. For children of 12 and under, Bowood offers a truly outstanding adventure playground, complete with life size pirate ship, giant slides, chutes and high level rope walks and the famous Space Dive. *Open daily, 27th Mar-31st Oct, 11am-6pm or dusk.* 01249 812102. www.bowood-estate.co.uk (See "Historic Sites" chapter and Advert page 50.)

C5 ⓔ Schools 🐦

Longleat Safari Park, **Warminster,** just off the A362 between Warminster and Frome. Come and enjoy Britain's first Safari Park. See the magnificent wildlife in natural surroundings and be as close as anyone can get to lions, tigers, rhinos, giraffes, elephants and many other species. Other Longleat attractions include Longleat House (open all year, see "Historic Sites" chapter), Postman Pat Village, Tropical Butterfly Garden, Maze, Adventure Castle and a 25-seater, winch operated, helium balloon. Save money with a passport ticket to all attractions or pay as you go. *Open daily 13th Mar-31st Oct, 10am-6pm. Last admission 5.30pm or dusk if earlier.* 01985 844400. www.longleat.co.uk (See Advert on page 50.)

ⓒ Schools — Open all year

Rode Bird Gardens, near **Bath,** home for over 200 species of birds, some flying freely through the trees. There is a miniature steam railway (Summer only, pay per ride), adventure playground and restaurant. *Open daily, 10am-6pm (dusk in Winter). Closed 25th Dec.* 01373 830326.

ⓑ Schools — Open all year

The Woodland Park and Heritage Centre, Brokerswood, near Westbury. The 80 acres of woodland offer nature trails, a lake with wildfowl, picnic and barbecue areas and a tea room. Narrow gauge railway, an indoor soft play area and two excellent adventure playgrounds. *Open daily, 10am-dusk.* 01373 822238.

D1 ⓑ Schools 🐦

Sleepy Hollow Farm Park, Blockley, just off the A44, near Moreton-in-Marsh. Take a woodland walk, find the Hidden Picnic Area or visit the indoor Pet Centre. Children will love the Animal Park with its walk-in pens. Also a 'farm' exclusively for birthday parties. *Open daily, end Mar-end Oct, 10.30am-6pm.* 01386 701264.

D2 ⓒ Schools — Open all year

Birdland, Rissington Road, **Bourton-on-the-Water.** Find birds from around the world in 7 acres of parkland. Attractive playground, pets corner and coffee shop. *Open daily, Apr-Oct, 10am-6pm, Nov-Mar, 10am-4pm. Last admission 1 hr. before closing.* 01451 820480.

ⓑ Schools

Cotswold Falconry Centre, Moreton-in-Marsh, just off A44, adjacent to Batsford Arboretum, is a small birds of prey centre housing hawks, owls, eagles and falcons. Four flying displays daily, weather permitting, with informative commentaries. Children are encouraged to help fly the birds whenever possible. *Open 1st Mar-30th Nov, daily, 10.30am-5pm.* 01386 701043.

Map Ref: Please refer to map on page 2.
Price Codes for a family of four: Ⓐ: less than £5 Ⓑ: £5-£10 Ⓒ: £10-£15 Ⓓ: £15-£20 Ⓔ: £20-£30 Ⓖ:- Over £30 Ⓕ: Free
Schools: Range of educational opportunities available. 🐦 Birthday parties organised.

9

MAP REFS
 PRICE CODES

D2

ⓑ Schools
🎈

Cotswold Farm Park, Guiting Power, is situated on one of the highest points of the area and was Britain's first ever farm park. It is home to a fascinating collection of rare breeds of British farm animals including heavily wooled Cotswold sheep, various cattle, Gloucester Old Spot pigs, goats, horses, poultry and waterfowl. Children can enter the Touch Barn and Pets Corner and are encouraged to stroke and feed the tame, hand reared baby animals. The adventure playground and bumps and hollows of the attractive picnic area are guaranteed to wear out the most energetic junior members of the family. Tea room and gift shop. *Open 20th Mar-31st Oct, daily 10.30am-5pm, Suns, Bank Hols and daily in Aug, 10.30am-6pm.* 01451 850307. (See Advert page 50.)

ⓑ Schools
Open all year
🎈

Folly Farm, Bourton-on-the-Water. The good, the bad and the ugly of domestic waterfowl and rare poultry can be fed on the lakes and in the grounds. Undercover small pets area where you can see and stroke rabbits, calves and ducklings. Lavender Fields will be in full bloom from July. *Open Summer, daily 10am-6pm, Winter, daily 10am-5pm.* 01451 820285.

D3

ⓑ Schools
Open all year

The Butts Farm, South Cerney, Cirencester, is a small family-run farm, specialising in rare breeds. Help bottle feed the animals, ride on a tractor or pony around the farm. Small playground with pirate ship for younger children and a farmyard nursery. *Open Easter-31st Oct, Wed-Sun, 11am-5pm (all week in school hols) and Sun all Winter.* 01285 862205.

ⓑ Schools
Open all year
🎈

Trout Farm, Bibury. There is something hypnotic about watching the tranquil pond waters come to life as you feed the trout on this working farm. Picnic area beside the River Coln. Groups by arrangement. *Open Summer, Mon-Sat, 9am-6pm, Sun 10am-6pm, Winter, Mon-Sat, 9am-5pm, Sun, 10am-5pm.* 01285 740215.

Map Ref: Please refer to map on page 2.
Price Codes for a family of four: Ⓐ: less than £5 Ⓑ: £5-£10 Ⓒ: £10-£15 Ⓓ: £15-£20 Ⓔ: £20-£30 Ⓖ:- Over £30 Ⓕ: Free
Schools: Range of educational opportunities available. 🎈 Birthday parties organised.

FREE PLACES

This chapter includes museums, a selection of parks, open spaces and other places that freely offer family entertainment and enjoyment. Although free admission, there may be some car parking charges, extra charges for schools and special activities, or requests for donations.

MAP REFS

A4 | *Open all year*
Ashcombe Park, Weston-super-Mare. is located 1 mile from the town centre between Upper Bristol Road and Milton Road. There is a children's recreation ground, grass and hard tennis courts, pitch and putting.

Schools
Open all year
Bristol International Airport, Lulsgate on the A38. From the café, you can watch planes landing and taking off and enjoy the general bustle of an airport. 01275 474444.

Clarence Park, Weston-super-Mare. At the southern end of Weston close to the seafront, this park has a children's recreation area.

Grand Pier, Weston-super-Mare. A traditional pier with covered amusement park, family fun deck and plenty of fresh air! Suitable for all ages. *Open Mar-Nov, Mon-Fri, 10am-5.30pm, Sat & Sun, 10am-7pm.* 01934 620238.

Open all year
Lake Grounds, Portishead, on the seafront, has tennis courts, a putting green, a lake for model boat sailing and a fenced children's playground.

Open all year
Weston Woods, Weston-super-Mare. 360 acres of woodland on Worlebury Hill overlooking Weston. Numerous paths, trails and an ancient British Hill Fort.

A5 | *Open all year*
Apex Leisure & Wildlife Park, off Marine Drive, Highbridge. An attractive park with a lake and fenced children's playground with swings, a slide and climbing frame.

Open all year
Cheddar Gorge. A dramatic limestone gorge with towering cliffs. Best approached from the N, via the B3371 and B3135. For further information telephone 01934 744071.

Open all year
Crosses Pen Park, Manor Gardens, Burnham-on-Sea. Close to the beach this park has a children's playground with swings, slide, roundabout and climbing frame. There are also tennis courts and an 18 hole putting course.

Glastonbury Tribunal, High Street, is a medieval building that now houses the Tourist Information Centre and has a garden for picnics. 01458 832949.

King John's Hunting Lodge, The Square, Axbridge. This late medieval merchants house occupies an important site at the corner of the High Street and Market Square. Now run as a local history museum, there is plenty of interest, including the original oak staircase. *Open Apr-Sept, daily, 2-5pm.* 01934 732012.

Open all year
Southwell Gardens, near Market Street, Highbridge. While older children can play five-a-side or netball on pitches that are open to the public, younger members of the family will enjoy the children's playground with swings, slide, climbing frame and roundabout.

B2 | *Open all year*
Forest of Dean, Cinderford. The forest stretches from close to the Welsh border in the W to Lydney near the River Severn in the E and Mitcheldean in the N. There are many trails, tracks, cycle routes and nature reserves in the forest. The famous Sculpture Trail - giant sculptures that can be climbed upon along a woodland track - starts from Beechenhurst Lodge on the B4226.

Map Ref: Please refer to map on page 2.

Schools: Range of educational opportunities available. ● Birthday parties organised.

B3 *Open all year* **Aust Wharf,** Old Passage Road, off the A403. While the original car ferry site is now derelict and overgrown, the quiet stretch of road leading to it is ideal for viewing both Severn Crossings.

Open all year **Coaley Peak Picnic Site,** 2 miles N of Uley on the B4066 and just across the road from the entrance to **Woodchester Mansion** (see "Historic Sites" chapter), this 12 acre site offers panoramic views over the Severn Vale, and adjoins a National Trust nature reserve complete with topograph.

Schools **Heritage Centre and Museum,** The Chipping, **Wotton-under-Edge.**
Open all year Located in a converted fire station, this friendly Centre offers much information of local interest. The museum has many intriguing artefacts, and changing displays. Groups by arrangement. *Open Summer, Tues-Sat, 10am-1pm, 2-5pm, and first Sun in the month, 2-5pm. Winter, closes 4pm.* 01453 521541.

Open all year **Mundy Playing Fields,** Thornbury. Large open area with playground, football pitches, tennis courts and children's paddling pool.

Schools **Oldbury Power Station,** Oldbury-on-Severn. A multi-media experience introduces you to the world of nuclear power at the Visitor Centre. Tours take about 1hr. Also walk around the nature trail *Open Summer, daily, 10am-4pm, last tour 3pm. Telephone for Winter opening times.* 01454 419899.

Woodchester Park, near **Nympsfield,** NT. Around 5 miles S of Stroud and 2 miles N of Uley on the B4066 this beautiful park is ideal for walking and picnics. 01453 860531.

B4 *Open all year* **Alice Park,** Bath. At the junction of A46 and the London Road, this park has a huge circular sandpit with diggers in the large play area, particularly suitable for children under 10. There are also tennis courts.

Open all year **Ashton Court,** Bristol. Near the Clifton Suspension Bridge, this Estate provides 850 acres of parks and woodland with something for everyone. Nature trails to pitch 'n' putt and a miniature railway. Various events are held in the Summer. 0117 9639174.

Open all year **Blaise Castle Estate,** Henbury, **Bristol,** comprises 400 acres of wood and parkland with paths and trails. There is also a children's playground and a miniature railway in the Summer. 0117 9506789.

Schools **Blaise Castle House Museum,** Henbury, Bristol. Set in the Blaise Castle
Open all year Estate, the 18th century building houses the social history collection of the City of Bristol Museum. *Open 1st Apr-31st Oct, Sat-Wed, 10am-5pm.* 0117 9506789.

Open all year **Brandon Hill,** Bristol. The cone-shaped hill is said to be the oldest park in Bristol. It is topped by the Cabot Tower from which there is a panoramic view of the city. There is a small nature reserve and children's playground.

Open all year **Castle Park,** Bristol. Set around the remains of a mediaeval castle, close to the city centre, children can explore the "castle" playground or search for pieces of artwork, including a carved stone throne.

Open all year **The Downs,** Clifton, Bristol. Huge expanse of open space for walking, ball games and flying kites. There is a small playground near the Suspension Bridge.

Open all year **Eastville Park,** Bristol. A large park with a boating lake and playground. It is also the starting point for the Frome Valley nature trail.

Open all year **Leigh Woods,** near Abbot's Leigh, **Bristol.** The car park is located off the A369 Bristol to Portishead road. The woods incorporate the Avon Gorge Nature Reserve and an ancient British Hill Fort. Spectacular views of the Avon Gorge.

Map Ref: Please refer to map on page 2.

Schools: Range of educational opportunities available. ● Birthday parties organised.

B4 Open all year **Owen Square,** Barton Hill, **Bristol,** has a large children's play area.

Schools
Open all year **Royal Victoria Park** is the largest park in **Bath.** The children's play area is laid out to look like the city itself. There is also an approach golf course, a boating lake for model boats and tennis courts.

Open all year **St. Georges, Bristol.** Roller skating and skateboarding are specially catered for in this park. There is also a boating lake and playground.

Open all year **Sydney Gardens** is the oldest park in **Bath.** The Chinese-style bridges across the Kennet and Avon Canal are an attraction. There are also tennis courts.

Open all year **Vassal Park,** off Fishponds Rd, **Bristol.** Part of the Frome Valley Walk, this extensive Park is ideal for walks and picnics. Large children's play area with some climbing equipment set on sand.

Schools
Open all year **Victoria Art Gallery,** Bridge Street, **Bath,** houses a collection of oil paintings and watercolours from European Old Masters to contemporary prints. Workshops held regularly. *Open Tues-Fri, 10am-5.30pm, Sat, 10am-5pm and Sun, 2-5pm, last admission half hour before closing, closed 25th-26th Dec, Mons and Bank Hols.* 01225 477772.

Willsbridge Mill Countryside and Education Centre, alongside the Siston Brook, has many wildlife habitats to be explored. Find out how to attract birds, bees and butterflies to your own garden. There is an exhibition centre which is *open Easter-end Sept, daily (except Mons & Sats), Bank Hols & Sun pm in Feb, Mar & Oct.* Discovery days are held during school hols. 0117 932 9440.

Schools
Open all year **Windmill Hill City Farm,** Bedminster, **Bristol.** A working farm, community garden, nature conservation area and adventure playground. *Open Tues-Sun, 9am-5pm, closed Bank Hol Mons.* Groups by appointment. 0117 9633252.

B5 Open all year **The Mendips.** Ideal for walking with views across the Bristol Channel to the mountains of Wales. Much evidence of early man and the Romans.

C2 Open all year **Chedworth Woods,** Chedworth, near Cheltenham. Good walks in extensive woodland near Roman villa and along disused railway track.

Schools
Open all year **Cheltenham Art Gallery and Museum,** Clarence Street. Well-planned discovery sheets in each gallery encourage children really to look at the exhibits that cover the archaeological, craft and social history of the area. A small gallery is devoted to the life of Edward Wilson who was on Scott's fateful 2nd Antarctic Expedition. *Open Mon-Sat, 10am-5.20pm. Closed Bank Hols.* 01242 237431.

Open all year **Crickley Hill Country Park,** 6 miles E of **Gloucester.** 144 acres of woodland and parkland on the edge of the Cotswold escarpment. There are the remains of an ancient hill fort and well-marked trails. 01452 863170.

Open all year **Gloucester Park,** Parkend Road, **Gloucester.** A central park, site of the fair and carnival in Summer. Bandstand, large children's play area and tennis courts.

The Little Museum, Church Street, **Tewkesbury.** Medieval timber-framed house, carefully restored to show the construction of a merchant's shop and house. *Open Easter-Nov, Tues-Sat, including Bank Hols, 10am-5pm.*

Open all year **Montpellier Gardens,** Cheltenham. Formal lawns and flower beds, but with a children's play area and tennis courts.

Open all year **Odda's Chapel,** EH, Deerhurst, near **Tewkesbury.** This Saxon chapel is unusually attached to a half-timbered farmhouse. Partly rebuilt and restored, for many years it lay undiscovered.

Free Places

Map Ref: Please refer to map on page 2.

Schools: Range of educational opportunities available. 🕯 Birthday parties organised.

C2

Open all year **Pittville Park,** Cheltenham, is a large attractive park with some of the finest aspects of Regency Cheltenham, ornamental lakes and gardens, as well as a children's play area, boating lake, approach golf and tennis courts.

Schools
Open all year **Robinswood Hill Country Park,** 2 miles S of **Gloucester.** 260 acres of countryside with marked nature and geology trails. It is also the site of the Gloucester Wildlife Trust Centre who organise visits for schools and a programme of discovery days during the school Summer holidays. 01452 303206..

Schools
Open all year **Tewkesbury Abbey,** Church Street. An impressive building with plenty of interest and well informed displays. Daily tours as shown on porch notice board. Groups by arrangement. *Open every Sun, 7.30am-7pm; Summer, Mon-Sat, 7.30am-5pm, Winter, Mon-Fri, 7.30am-5.30pm, Sat, 7.30am-4.30pm.* 01684 850959.

Westgate Leisure Area, St Oswalds Road, **Gloucester.** There is a lake and 9 hole pitch & putt course open from Apr-Sept only. There are also picnic benches and riverside walks.

Wishing Fish Clock, Regent Arcade, **Cheltenham.** A crowd gathers each half hour to watch this intriguing clock spring into action. The monster fish blow bubbles, catch one and you can make a wish!

C3

Open all year **Athelstan Museum,** Town Hall, Cross Hayes, **Malmesbury.** There are displays of local history including lace-making, costumes and early bicycles together with illustrations of old Malmesbury. *Open Apr-Sept, Tues-Sun, 10.30am-12.30pm, 1-3pm; Oct-Mar, check for Winter opening times.* 01666 823748.

Open all year **Cirencester Lock-up,** Trinity Road. Built in the days before police stations, this is one of only a few preserved lock-ups in England. It is now part of the Cotswold Council Headquarters. *Open Mon-Fri, office hours.* Other times, key held at the Corinium Museum (see "Historic Sites" chapter). 01285 655611.

Open all year **Keynes Country Park,** 4 miles S of **Cirencester.** Lakeside park with walks, barbecues, trim trail, playground, children's beach and nature reserve. Parking charges in the Summer.

Open all year **Minchinhampton and Rodborough Commons,** NT, 200 acres, very popular for kite flying and picnics.

Open all year **St Michael's Park,** off Kings Street, **Cirencester.** Attractive, well-kept park with two play areas, one with swings, slides and sandpits and the other a small, rustic adventure trail. There are also tennis courts, mini and crazy golf and croquet. Barbecues can be hired during the Summer months. 01285 659182.

Open all year **Stratford Park,** Stroud, has woodland walks, duck pond, bandstand and children's play area adjoining the Leisure Centre (see "Activities" chapter).

 C4

Open all year **Barton Farm Countryside Park,** Bradford-on-Avon. Set in the wooded valley of the River Avon, the park is flanked by the river and the Kennet and Avon Canal, with plenty of walks. There is a well-preserved Tithe Barn, a 14th century building maintained by English Heritage.

Schools
Open all year **Bradford-on-Avon Museum,** Bridge Street, displays the heritage of the local region. The centrepiece is a rebuilt 120 year old pharmacy shop. *Open Apr-Oct, Wed-Sat, 10.30am-12.30pm, 2-4pm; Sun, 2-4pm; Nov-Mar, Wed-Fri and Sat 2-4pm, Sat, 10.30am-12.30pm, 2-4pm; Bank Hol Mons, 2-4pm; closed Christmas.* 01225 863280.

Open all year **John Coles Park,** Fleet Road, **Chippenham.** There are bowls, tennis courts, a fenced-in play area and plenty of open space for games.

Yelde Hall Museum, Market Place, **Chippenham.** An exhibition of local history housed in a 16th century yelde hall with a 15th century council chamber and lock-up. *Open mid Mar-31st Oct, Mon-Sat, 10am-12.30pm, 2-4.30pm. Closed Bank Hols.* 01249 651488.

C5 | *Open all year* — **Lake Pleasure Grounds,** off Weymouth Street, **Warminster.** There is a large boating lake, fed by the River Were, tennis courts, putting green, paddling pool and an adventure playground.

Schools *Open all year* — **Trowbridge Museum,** The Shires, Court Street, tells the story of a West Country woollen town, its history and people using reconstructions including a weaver's cottage and draper's shop. *Open Tues-Fri, 10am-4pm, Sat, 10am-5pm.* 01225 751339.

Open all year — **Trowbridge Park,** Park Road, is West Wiltshire's largest park. It has a popular play area, crazy golf course and hardcourt, suitable for volleyball, basketball and hockey. The adjoining Civic Hall has catering facilities.

D3 | *Open all year* — **Coate Water Country Park,** Swindon. The park surrounds a large boating/fishing lake. There is pitch and putt, miniature golf, picnic and barbecue areas, a paddling pool and a large dog-free area with sandpit and play equipment. A nature and wildlife reserve has bird hides. 01793 490150.

Open all year — **Cotswold Water Park,** Ashton Keynes, incorporating the **Keynes** and **Neigh Bridge Country Parks** include over 80 lakes with lakeside walks, children's beach, paddling area, picnic sites and nature reserves. There are seasonal facilities for water sports, fishing and camping. 01285 861459.

Open all year — **Lydiard Park,** Swindon. There are farmland and woodland walks, nature trails, a visitors' centre with exhibitions and extensive and exciting play areas for children. *Open Mon-Sat, 10am-1pm, 2pm-dusk, Sun, 2pm-dusk.* 01793 771419.

Open all year — **Neigh Bridge Country Park,** Somerford Keynes, has lakeside walks, children's playground and picnic site. 01285 861459.

Schools *Open all year* — **Swindon Museum and Art Gallery,** Bath Road. There are displays of local history, archaeology and geology and collections of old instruments, spears and some items to handle. See the sea dragons of Swindon and find the life size Gharial! The gallery houses a collection of 20th century British art. *Open Mon-Sat, 10am-5.30pm, Sun, 2-5.30pm, closed Bank Hols.* 01793 466559.

Open all year — **Town Gardens,** Quarry Road, **Swindon,** is an ornamental park alongside which there is a children's play area and tennis courts.

D4 | *Open all year* — **Avebury Stone Circle,** NT, **Avebury.** This village is set within the famous megalithic stone circle. You can walk around the stones and avenue of megaliths. Car parking outside village with a place for picnics.

Schools *Open all year* — **Barbury Castle Country Park,** near **Wroughton.** Dramatic scenery and ancient trackways include The Ridgeway National Trail, taking you along one of the oldest roads in the world. Groups by arrangement. 01793 845346.

Open all year — **Savernake Forest,** Marlborough. Once a royal hunting forest, there are 2,300 acres of woodland, rides and open glades, with deer still to be seen. There are plenty of walks and trails to follow.

DIRECTORY OF ACTIVITIES AND INFORMATION

CONTENTS

General abbreviations used in addresses within the listings are as follows: Ave.: Avenue, Clo.: Close, Cresc.: Crescent, Dri.: Drive, Gdns.: Gardens, Gr.: Green, Gro.: Grove, La.: Lane, Pk.: Park, Pl.: Place, R.G.: Recreation Ground, Rd.: Road, Sq.: Square, St.: Street, Tce.: Terrace.
✦: Birthday Party

Abbreviations specific to a particular section are listed at the beginning of that section.

ADVENTURE PLAY CENTRES

A4 ✦ **Weston-super-Mare**, Kidscove, Searle Cresc. 01934 417411.

B4 ✦ **Bristol**, Alphabet Zoo, Winterstoke Rd. 0117 9663366.

✦ **Planet Kids**, Arena One, Brunel Way. 0117 9538538.

C2 ✦ **Cheltenham**, Ballyhoo, Chosen View Rd. 01242 252205.

BOAT HIRE

Abbreviations: C: Canoes, M: Motor boats, P: Pedalos, R: Rowing boats, SE: Self drive electric boats.

B4 **Bath**, Bath Boating Station, Forester Rd. Punts, canoes and rowing boats. 01225 466407. (See also "Trips" chapter and Advert page 6.)

Bathford. C. R. and skiffs. 01225 859847.
Bristol, City Docks. R. 0117 9268157.
Kennet and Avon Canal. Self drive electric boats can be hired by the hour or day from near the Dundas Aquaduct. 01225 722292.
Willsbridge, Avon Valley Country Park. R. 0117 9864929.

C2 **Cheltenham**, Pittville Park. C. P. R.
Tewkesbury, M and day boats operate between Easter and end Oct. 01684 294088.

C4 **Semington**, The Lock House. SE. *Easter-Oct.* 01380 870654.

C5 **Warminster**, Lake Pleasure Grounds. R.

D3 **Ashton Keynes**, Cotswold Water Park. C. 01285 861202.
Lechlade, River Thames. M. R. 01367 253599.

BOWLING (TEN PIN)

A4 ✦ **Weston-super-Mare**, AMF Bowling, Carlton St. 01934 626480.

B4 ✦ **Bristol**, Arena One, Superbowl, Brunel Way, Ashton Gate. 0117 9538538.

C2 ✦ **Cheltenham**, Cotswold Bowl, 2 Wymans La, Kingsditch. 01242 226766.

✦ **Gloucester**, Minnesota Fats Sports Bar, The Peel Centre. 01452 414962 (Day time only.)

C4 ✦ **Melksham**, Christie Miller SC, 32 Lancaster Rd., Bowerhill. 01225 702826.

D3 ✦ **Fairford**, Skytanker Lanes. 01285 714444.

✦ **Swindon**, Swindon Super Bowl, Whitehill Way. 01793 886886.

CINEMAS

A4 **Clevedon**, Curzon, Old Church Rd. 01275 871000.
Weston-super-Mare, Odeon, The Centre. 01934 642378 / 08705 050007.

A5 **Burnham-on-Sea**, Ritz Cinema, Victoria St. 01278 782871.

B3 **Wotton-under-Edge**, Town Cinema, 01453 845533 / 521666.

B4 **Bath**, ABC, 23/24 Westgate St. 01225 462959/461730. **Little Theatre**, St Michael's Pl. 01225 466822. **Robins Cinema**, St John's Pl. 01225 461506.
Bristol, ABC, Whiteladies Rd. 0117 9733640. **Arts Centre**, Kings Sq, Kingsdown. 0117 9240195. **Cineworld**, Hengrove. 01275 831099. **Odeon**, Union St. 08705 050007. **Orpheus**, Henleaze. 0117 9621644. **Showcase**, St. Philips

Map Ref: Please refer to map on page 2.   ✦ Birthday parties organised.

16

B4 Causeway. 0117 9723434. **Warner Village,** The Venue, Cribbs Causeway. 0117 9500222. **Watershed Media Centre,** 1 Canons Rd. 0117 9276444.

B5 **Frome,** Westway Cinema, Cork St. 01373 465685.
Wells, New Wells Film Centre, Princes Rd. 01749 672036.

C2 **Cheltenham,** Odeon, Winchcombe St. 01242 261800 / 08705 050007.
Gloucester, Virgin Cinemas, The Peel Centre, St Ann Way, Bristol Rd. 0541 555174.

C3 **Cirencester,** Regal Cinema, Lewis La. 01285 658755/652358.

C4 **Chippenham,** Astoria Cinema, Marshfield Rd. 01249 652498.
Devizes, The Palace Cinema, The Market Place. 01380 722971.

D3 **Swindon,** Virgin Cinemas, Shaw Ridge Leisure Pk. 0541 555174. **Cineworld,** Greenbridge Retail Centre. 01793 420710.

ICE SKATING

B4 **Bristol,** John Nike Leisuresport Ltd, Bristol Ice Rink, Frogmore St. 0117 9292148.

D3 **Swindon,** The Link Centre, Whitehill Way, Westlea. 01793 445566.

KARTING

A4 **Portishead,** The Raceway, Unit 4, Parish Wharf Trading Est., Harbour Rd. 01275 817011.

B4 **Bristol,** Bristol Karting Centre, 214-224 Broomhill Rd. Brislington. 0117 9770600.

C2 **Gloucester,** Karting Centre, 5 Madleaze Ind. Est., Bristol Rd. 01452 311211.

C3 **Cirencester,** Water Parks, Lake 11, Spine Rd. 01285 861345.

C4 **Hullavington,** Go-Karting Leiṣure Services. 01249 446503.

D3 **Swindon,** Winners Karting, Churchward Village, Kemble Dr. 01793 430736.

LASER FUN

A4 **Weston-super-Mare,** Mr B's Amusements, 12-20 Regent St. 01934 629683.

B4 **Bath,** Quasar Centre, Ambury Warehouse, Corn St. 01225 463311.
Bristol, Harry's Quasar Centre. 0117 9277671. **Laser Quest,** Silver St, Broadmead. 0117 9496688.

LOCAL COUNCILS

Bath and North East Somerset County Council	01225 477000
Bristol City Council	0117 9222000
Gloucestershire County Council	01452 425000
North West Somerset County Council	01934 888888
Somerset County Council	01823 355455
South Gloucestershire County Council	01454 868686
Wiltshire County Council	01225 713000

PITCH & PUTT

A4 **Portishead,** Portishead Pitch 'n' Putt, Nore Rd. 9 hole course. 01934 888888.
Weston-super-Mare, Ashcombe Park. 01934 627329.

B4 **Bath,** Approach Golf Course, Western Rd. 12 & 18 hole. 01225 331162.
Bristol, Ashton Court Estate, Clifton Lodge entrance. 18 hole course. 0117 9738508.

C2 **Cheltenham,** Pittville Park. 18 hole course. 01242 528764.
Gloucester, Ski Centre, Matson La. 9 hole course. 01452 414300.

C4 **Chippenham,** Monkton Park.
Melksham, Christie Miller Sports Centre. 01225 702826.

D3 **Highworth,** Community Golf Centre, Swindon Rd. 01793 766014.
Swindon, Coate Water Country Park; Moredon Playing Fields. 01793 522837.

PUTTING GREENS

A4 **Portishead,** Lake Grounds Park. 01934 888888.
Weston-super-Mare, Ashcombe Park. **Beach Lawns,** Park Pl. 01934 627329.

A5 **Burnham-on-Sea,** Crosses Pen Park.

B4 **Bath,** Combe Manor Grove Hotel, Brassnocker Hill, Monkton Combe. Also driving range and 5 hole practice course. 01225 835533. **Royal Victoria Park.** 01225 425066.

C2 **Gloucester,** Westgate Leisure Area, St. Oswalds Rd.
Tewkesbury, Sherdon's Golf Course, Manor Farm, Tredington. 01684 274782.

C3 **Cirencester,** St Michaels Park, off Kings St.

C5 **Stroud,** Stratford Park.

Map Ref: Please refer to map on page 2.   ◆ Birthday parties organised.

17

C5 **Trowbridge**, Trowbridge Park.
Warminster, Lake Pleasure Grounds. 01985 212047.

D3 **Highworth**, Community Golf Centre.
Swindon, Coate Water Country Park. Also crazy golf. **Penhill Park**.

QUAD BIKE

C3 ✦**Cirencester**, Water Parks, Lake 11, Spine Rd. 01285 861345.

SKIING

A5 **Sandford**, Avon Ski Centre, Lyncombe Lodge, Lyncombe Dr. 01934 852828.

C2 **Gloucester**, Ski Centre, Matson La. 01452 414300.

SOFT PLAY AREAS

A4 **Portishead**, Parish Wharf Leisure Centre, 01275 848494.

B3 **Thornbury**, Leisure Centre, Alveston Hill. 01454 865777.

B4 **Bristol**, Explorers of the Lost World, 39 Brislington Hill. 0117 9831343.
Little Stoke, Maritime Mayhem, Harriers Fitness Club. 01454 888666.
Yate, Leisure Centre, Kennedy Way. 01454 8658000.

C2 **Gloucester**, Trumbleland, Barton St. 01452 307771. **PlayZone**, Riverside Sports & Leisure Centre, St. Oswald's Rd. 01452 413214.

C5 **Brokerswood**, near Westbury, Woodland Park and Heritage Museum. 01373 822238.

D3 **Swindon**, South Marston Arms and Leisure Club, Sandy La., South Marston. 01793 827777.

SPORTS AND LEISURE CENTRES

Abbreviations: LC: Leisure Centre, RC: Recreation Centre, SC: Sports Centre, SH: Sports Hall.

*: Centre has a swimming pool.

† "Dual use" system, i.e. schools use the facilities during the day and the centres become available to the general public from early evening during the week, at weekends and throughout the school holidays.

A4 **Backwell**, Backwell LC*, Farleigh Rd. 01275 463726.
Churchill, Churchill SC*, Churchill Green. 01934 852303.

A4 ✦**Clevedon**, Clevedon SC †, Valley Rd. ✦01275 877182. **Strode LC***, Strode Way. 01275 879242.
✦**Nailsea**, Scotch Horn LC, Brockway. 01275 856965.
✦**Portishead**, Parish Wharf LC*, 01275 848494.
✦**Weston-super-Mare**, Hutton Moor*, Hutton Moor Rd. 01934 635347.

A5 ✦**Cheddar**, Kings of Wessex LC*, Station Rd. 01934 744939.

B2 ✦**Cinderford**, Heywood SC*†, Causeway Rd. 01594 824008.
✦**Coleford**, Five Acres LC*†, Berry Hill. 01594 835388.
Newent, Newent LC*†, Watery La. 01531 821519.

B3 **Dursley**, SC†, Kings Hill. 01453 543832.
✦**Lydney**, Whitecross SC†, Church Rd. 01594 842383.
✦**Thornbury**, Thornbury LC*, Alveston Hill. 01454 865777.

B4 ✦**Bath**, Bath S & LC*, North Parade Rd. ✦01225 462563. **Culverhay SC***†, Rush Hill. 01225 480882.
Bristol, Bradley Stoke SC, opening mid 1999. **Easton** LC*†, 0117 9558840. **Greenway SC**, Doncaster Rd. 0117 ✦9503335. **Horfield SC**, Dorian Rd. 0117 ✦9521650. **Kingsdown SC**, Portland St. ✦0117 9426582. **Robin Cousins SC**, West Town Rd. 0117 9823514.
✦**Keynsham**, Keynsham LC*, Temple St. 0117 9861274.
✦**Whitchurch**, Whitchurch SC, Bamfield. 01275 8377822.
✦**Yate**, LC*, Kennedy Way. 01454 865800.

B5 ✦**Frome**, Frome SC*, Princess Anne Rd. 01373 465446.
✦**Midsomer Norton**, South Wansdyke SC*, Rackvernal Rd. 01761 415522.
✦**Shepton Mallet**, Shepton Mallet LC, Charlton Rd. 01749 346644.
✦**Wells**, Wells LC*, Charter Way. 01749 670055.

C2 ✦**Cheltenham**, Cleeve SC†, Twohedges Rd, Bishops Cleeve. 01242 673581.
✦**Cheltenham** RC*, Tommy Taylor's La. 01242 528764.
✦**Gloucester**, Brockworth SC*†, Mill La. 01452 863518. **Churchdown SC†**, Winston Rd. 01452 855994. **Gloucester LC***, Bruton Way. 01452 306498.

Map Ref: Please refer to map on page 2. ✦ Birthday parties organised.

18

Directory of Activities & Information

MAP REFS	

C3 ✦**Cirencester**, Cotswold LC*, Tetbury Rd. 01285 654057.

Stroud, Stratford Park LC*, Stratford Rd. 01453 766771.

Tetbury, Tetbury SLC†, Sir William Romney School, Lowfield Rd. 01666 505805.

Tewkesbury, Tewkesbury SC*†, Ashchurch Rd, Newtown. 01684 293953.

C4 **Calne**, White Horse LC*†, White Horse Way. 01249 814032.

✦**Chippenham**, The Olympiad LC*, Monkton Park. 01249 444144.

✦**Corsham**, Springfield SC*†, Beechfield Rd. 01249 712846.

✦**Devizes**, LC*†, Southbroom Rd. 01380 728894.

✦**Melksham**, Christie Miller SC, 32 Lancaster Rd., Bowerhill. 01225 702826.

C5 ✦**Trowbridge**, Castle Place LC, Level 5A, Multistorey Car Park, Castle St. 01225 762711. ✦**Trowbridge** SC*†, Frome Rd. 01225 764342.

✦**Warminster**, SC*†, Woodcock Rd. 01985 212946.

D3 **Cricklade**, LC*, Stones La. 01793 750011.

✦**Fairford**, Fairford SC† , Farmors School Campus. 01285 713786.

✦**Highworth**, The Rec*, (outdoor pool in the Summer months), The Elms. 01793 762602.

Swindon, Croft SC, Marlborough La., Old Town. 01793 526622. **The County Ground Lifestyle Complex**, County Rd. ✦01793 617782. **Haydon Centre**, Thames Ave, Haydon Wick. 01793 706666. **The** ✦**Link Centre***, Whitehill Way, Westlea. 01793 445566. **The Oasis LC***, North Star ✦ Ave. 01793 445401. **Park Youth and Community Centre**†, Marlowe Ave. 01793 521615.

D4 ✦**Marlborough** LC*, Barton Dean. 01672 513161.

Pewsey, SC*, 01672 562469.

✦**Wootton Bassett**, Lime Kiln LC*†. 01793 852197.

✦**Wroughton**, SC*†, Inverary Rd. 01793 813280.

SWIMMING POOLS (INDOOR)

Please also check the list of Sports & Leisure Centres above Those marked with an * have a pool.

A5 **Burnham-on-Sea**, Swimming Pool, Berrow Rd. 01278 785909.

B3 **Dursley**, Swimming Pool, Castle St. 01453 546441.

B4 **Bristol**, Bishopsworth Pool, Whitchurch Rd. 0117 9640258. **Bristol North Pool**, 98 Gloucester Rd., Bishopston. 0117 9243548. **Bristol South Pool**, Dean La., Bedminster. 0117 9663131. **Dolphin Pool**, Elm Park, Filton. 0117 9694542. **Filwood Swimming Pool**, Filwood Broadway, Knowle West. 0117 9662823. **Henbury Swimming Pool**, Crow La., Henbury. 0117 9500141. **Jubilee Pool**, Jubilee Rd., Knowle. 0117 9777900. **Shirehampton Pool**, Park Rd., Shirehampton. 0117 9822627. **Speedwell Pool**, Whitefield Rd., Speedwell. 0117 9674778.

Winterbourne, The Ridings High, High St. Evenings & Suns. 01454 772347.

C4 **Bradford-on-Avon**, Swimming Pool, St Margaret's St. 01225 862970.

Melksham, The Blue Pool, Market Pl. 01225 703525.

C5 **Westbury**, Swimming Pool, Church St. 01373 822891.

D3 **Swindon**, Health Hydro, Milton Rd. 01793 465630. **Dorcan Pool**, Dorcan School, St Paul's Dr. Evenings and weekends. 01793 533763.

SWIMMING POOLS (OUTDOOR)

A4 **Portishead**, Open Air Pool, Esplanade Rd. 01275 843454.

B3 **Wotton-under-Edge**, Symm Lane. 01453 842626.

C2 **Cheltenham**, The Lido, Sandford Open Air Pool, Keynsham Rd. 01242 524430.

C3 **Cirencester**, Open Air Baths, Tetbury Rd. 01285 653947.

Stroud, Stratford LC, Stratford Park. 01453 766771.

D3 **Highworth**, The Rec Outdoor Pool, The Elms. 01793 762602.

THEATRES

A4 **Weston-super-Mare**, Playhouse, High St. 01934 645544.

B4 **Bath**, Theatre Royal, St John's Pl. 01225 448844.

Bristol, Colston Hall, Colston St. 0117 9223682. **Hippodrome**, St Augustine's Parade. 0117 9299444. **Redgrave**, Percival

Map Ref: Please refer to map on page 2. ✦ Birthday parties organised.

19

B4 Rd., Clifton. 0117 9743384. **St George's,** Brandon Hill. 0117 9230359. **Theatre Royal,** (home of the Bristol Old Vic Theatre Company) King St. 0117 9264388.

B5 **Frome,** Merlin Theatre, Bath Rd. 01373 465949.

C2 ✦**Cheltenham,** Everyman, Regent St. 01242 572573. **Playhouse,** Bath Rd. 01242 522852.

Gloucester, Guildhall Arts Centre, 23 Eastgate St. 01452 505089. **New Olympus,** 162-166 Barton St. 01452 525917. **The King's Theatre,** 01452 300130.

Tewkesbury, Roses Theatre, Sun St. 01684 295074.

C3 **Cirencester,** Brewery Arts, Brewery Court. 01285 655522.

Stroud, Cotswold Playhouse, Parliament St. 01453 756379.

Uley, Prema Arts Centre, South St. 01453 860703.

C4 **Chippenham,** Theatre in the Downs, The Olympiad LC, Monkton Park. 01249 654970.

Devizes, Wharf Theatre. 01380 724741.

C5 **Warminster,** West Wiltshire Arts Centre. The Athenaeum, High St. 01985 213891/218519.

D3 **Swindon,** Arts Centre, Devizes Rd. 01793 614837. **Links Art Studio,** Link Centre, Whitehill Way. 01793 445566. **Wyvern Theatre,** Theatre Sq. 01793 524481.

TOURIST INFORMATION CENTRES

Bath, 01225 477101
Bradford-on-Avon, 01225 865797
Bristol, 0117 926 0767
Cheddar, 01934 744071
Cheltenham, 01242 522878
Chippenham, 01249 706333
Cirencester, 01285 654180
Coleford, 01594 812388
Devizes, 01380 729408
Frome, 01373 467271
Glastonbury, 01458 832954
Gloucester, 01452 421188
Malmesbury, 01666 823748
Marlborough, 01672 513989
Newent, 01531 822468
Swindon, 01793 530328
Trowbridge, 01225 777054
Warminster, 01985 218548
Wells, 01749 672552
Weston-super-Mare, 01934 626838

West Country Tourist Board, 01392 276351

WATER FUN PARKS

Centres with some wonderful features, maybe flumes, wave machines or rapids!

A4 **Weston-super-Mare,** Tropicana Pleasure Beach, Marine Parade. *Open May-Sept.* 01934 626581.

A5 **Brean,** Leisure Park, Coast Rd. Slide open Summer only. 01278 751595.

C2 **Tewkesbury,** Cascades, Oldbury Rd. 01684 293740.

C4 **Chippenham,** The Olympiad LC, Monkton Park. 01249 444144.

D3 **Swindon,** The Oasis LC, North Star Ave. 01793 445401.

WATERSPORTS

Abbreviations: C: Canoeing, J: Jet Skiing, K: Kayaking, S: Sailing, W: Windsurfing, WS: Waterskiing.

C3 **Cirencester,** Water Parks, Lake 11, Spine Rd. J. 01285 861345.

D3 **Ashton Keynes,** Cotswold Water Park. C. K. S. W.. 01285 861202.

Let's go to London

PRICE CODES

Let's take a trip

on the canal . . .

©/Ⓔ
Schools
Open all
year

↔
Camden Town

Canal Waterbus will enable you to see a side of London that you never knew existed. Boat trips run along the historic Regents Canal between Camden Lock and picturesque Little Venice, with its island, wildfowl and boats. The trips pass through Regents Park, where you can get off to visit the Zoo, and the Maida Hill Tunnel and can include a stop for lunch, a picnic or shopping. Excellent educational resources and special group rates. *Trips run daily Apr-Oct, weekends only Nov-Mar.* Information: 0171 482 2660. Bookings: 0171 482 2550.

on the River Thames . . .

The River Thames is "the thread which links the pearls of London's heritage and culture" and is a brilliant place from which to see some of London's treasures. There is no better way to enjoy the Thames than on board a riverboat. Evening cruises are running this year down the lower Thames specially to view either the Tower or the Millenium Dome but a new regular passenger service will be running in 2000, to enable you to travel in supreme comfort on new luxury boats from the South Bank near Waterloo to a special new pier at the Millenium Dome in Greenwich (see below).

Ⓓ
Open all
year

↔
Westminster
Tower Hill

From Westminster and from the Tower with **City Cruises**. Look out for the Red Fleet and take the children on a memorable cruise from Westminster to the Tower of London or vice versa. Enjoy the excellent views of the Houses of Parliament, Big Ben, St. Paul's Cathedral, Shakespeare's Globe, the Tower of London and the magnificent Tower Bridge whilst listening to an interesting commentary on all of the sights given by a member of the crew. Whichever pier you start your cruise from you will find several other attractions you may wish to visit, all within a short walking distance - many of them advertised in this feature. This Red Fleet is leading the way on the Thames into the Millenium with its flagship "Millenium of London". This super luxury craft is the model for the new fleet coming into service later this year in readiness for taking visitors down the river to the Millenium Dome at Greenwich non stop from the South Bank near Waterloo in the year 2000! Combined travel and entrance tickets to the Millenium Dome will be available for you to pre-book.
For 1999 boat services commence at 10.20am from Apr-Oct running at 20 min intervals and from Nov-Mar from 10.30am every 45 mins. Services run until 9pm Jun-Aug. Closed Christmas Day. 0171 930 8589. (See Advert page ii.)

Ⓓ/Ⓖ
↔
Westminster

From Westminster with **Westminster Passenger Service Association**. Take a boat trip upriver from Westminster and combine a leisurely cruise with a visit to either Kew Gardens, Richmond or Hampton Court. Sit back and enjoy an interesting commentary about the historic sights including views of Big Ben, the Houses of Parliament, Lambeth Palace and some of the major London bridges. Further upstream you will pass through some of the prettier stretches of the Thames, and view country estates and houses from your vantage point on the river. *Regular sailings from Mar-Sept, with a limited service Oct. Evening cruises run May-Sept to view the Tower of London or to view the Millenium Dome.* 0171 930 2062/4721. (See Advert page x).

on the Docklands Light Railway . . .

Ⓑ/©
Open all
year

↔
Tower Hill

Docklands Light Railway gives you easy access to London Docklands, one of the world's largest urban regeneration programmes which is transforming the former port area. Stunning modern architecture set amid historic docks, lots of activities, waterside shops and cafes are all worth seeing. Take the spectacular elevated skyline ride on the Railway from Tower Gateway station, opposite the Tower of London with easy connection to the London Underground network. See the Millenium Dome or Canary Wharf with its shops and restaurants, or stop off at Mudchute to visit the Park and Farm. From the end of the line, Island Gardens, take the Victorian foot tunnel under the Thames to enjoy the delights of Greenwich. A Docklander ticket is good value giving you a day's unlimited travel to explore the area. Travelcards are valid for use provided they cover the correct zones. Or, why not combine Docklands with Greenwich and a river boat trip with a "Sail & Rail" ticket available from Tower Gateway station or Westminster Pier. The ticket also gives you 20% off entry fee to the National Maritime Museum. 0171 363 9700 (24 hour answerphone). (See Advert page vi.)

Price Codes for a family of four: **Ⓐ**: less than £5 **Ⓑ**: £5-£10 **©**: £10-£15 **Ⓓ**: £15-£20 **Ⓔ**: £20-£30 **Ⓖ**: Over £30 **Ⓕ**: Free
Schools: Range of educational opportunities available. ♦ Birthday parties organised. ↔ Nearest tube station.

Let's Go to the Theatre

CATS, New London Theatre, Drury Lane, for a purrfect day out, is still leaping ahead after almost two decades! Andrew Lloyd Webber's family favourite is London and Broadway's longest running musical and, with a magical blend of fantasy, poetry and dance set in an all-singing and all-dancing giant playground of feline friends, will thrill an audience of any age. There are offers for groups of children and school parties which is good news for parents and teachers alike. Special children's party rates of £12.50 per person are available for matinee performances on Tuesdays or, alternatively, for £17.50 per person (groups over 10), a "Purrfect Day Out" includes a special backstage tour of the theatre followed by a packed lunch before taking seats for the Tuesday matinee. Tailor-made workshops can be arranged for individual groups by calling John Scarborough in the Education Office: 0171 400 5005 or e-mail CATSUK@csi.com (See Advert page xi.)

Ⓖ
Schools
Open all year

↔
Covent Garden

Disney's Beauty and the Beast©, Dominion Theatre, Tottenham Court Road, is a fantastic adaptation of one of the world's favourite love stories. A selfish prince is transformed into a beast by an evil enchantress and in order to break the spell the Beast must learn to love and to be loved in return, before the last petal of a magic rose falls to the ground. But who could ever learn to love a Beast? Can Belle, the Beauty, help? The show features the Academy Award® winning title theme plus new songs specially written for the stage. This lavish show, which has a cast of 40, with over 250 costumes and 120 wigs being used, is also the proud recipient of London's top Olivier Award and Broadway's prestigious Tony® Award. A spectacle indeed for all the family to enjoy. 0171 416 6072. (See Advert page iv and enter the Competition in this book to try and win some family tickets!)

Ⓖ
Schools
Open all year

↔
Tottenham Court Road

Doctor Dolittle, London Apollo Theatre, Queen Caroline Street, Hammersmith. Be ready for some wonderful surprises here and enjoy the breathtaking flight of the giant Lunar Moth as it flies over your heads! This is the only London Theatre big enough to accommodate such a spectacle and the theatre has been totally transformed into the stunning world of Doctor Dolittle. The wonderful musical event introduces 92 amazing animals created by the animatronics team responsible for enormous hit films such as 101 Dalmatians and Babe. Gub-Gub, the pig, Dab Dab, the duck and the renowned, two headed Pushmi-Pullyu are sure to delight and thrill children of all ages! School and group rates available, 0171 416 6075. All other enquiries, 0870 6063400. (See Advert page ii.)

Ⓖ
Schools
Open all year

↔
Hammersmith

Andrew Lloyd Webber's Starlight Express, Apollo Victoria Theatre, is like nothing you've ever seen before! This high velocity muscial pushes the roller-skating cast to the limit as they hurtle round the theatre at speeds topping 40 miles an hour. Fusing state of the art technology, electrifying songs and a dazzling set, Starlight Express is light years ahead - so climb aboard, fasten your seatbelts and get ready for two hours of speed, spectacle, thrills and spills. The whole family will love it! A pre-performance presentation designed to give an insight into a large scale musical and a resource pack with ideas for pre and post performance work is available to school parties. Call the Apollo Victoria Schools Hotline. 0171 828 7074. (See Advert page iv.)

Ⓖ
Schools
Open all year

↔
Victoria

Let's Play

Snakes and Ladders, Syon Park, **Brentford,** is well signposted from Syon Park or can be accessed via 237 or 267 bus from Kew Bridge BR or Gunnersbury Underground station. Children can find action packed fun whatever the weather. They can let off steam in the giant supervised indoor main playframe, intermediate 2-5s area or toddlers area or use the outdoor adventure playground when the sun shines. A mini motor bike circuit provides an exciting additional activity. Meanwhile parents can relax in the cafe overlooking the playframe. *Open daily 10am-6pm. Last admission 5.15pm.* All children must wear socks. 0181 847 0946.

Ⓑ
Schools
Open all year
Q
↔
Gunnersbury

Let's Visit

BBC EXPERIENCE, Broadcasting House, Portland Place, is one of the most innovative interactive exhibitions in London and is the undisputed home of TV and Radio. Go along and be a sports commentator, direct an episode of Eastenders or star in your very own radio play! Charting generations of BBC history, from black & white cartoons and classic comedies to forecasting the weather and playing with the latest CD-ROM technology, you can experience all this and more at the very home of entertainment. Live daily. Call now to book your tour: 0870 603 03 04 (calls are charged at national rate) or visit the website: www.bbc.co.uk/experience/ (See Advert page vi.)

Ⓔ Schools Open all year
↔ Oxford Circus

HMS Belfast, off Morgans Lane, Tooley Street, is just a short walk from Tower Bridge. A real voyage of discovery awaits you here and will enthrall you and your children. HMS Belfast is the only surviving example of the great fleets of big gun armoured warships built for the Navy in the first half of this century. There is much to explore in the 187 metres of her length. You will encounter steep ladders and narrow passages when travelling from deck to deck and on the way you will see the sick bay and officers' cabins, the chapel, boiler and engine rooms, punishment rooms, the Captain's bridge, the gun decks and more. Children will love the adventure here, but they must be supervised and care must be taken when using the ship's ladders. Not suitable for infants and disabled persons. Schools facilities: contact the Education Officer Jo Hunt. *Open daily except Christmas period 24th-26th Dec, 10am-6pm (last admission 5.15pm), closes 5pm in Winter (last admission 4.15pm).* 0171 940 6300. (See Advert page vi.)

Ⓒ Schools Open all year
↔ Tower Hill London Bridge

Kew Bridge Steam Museum, Green Dragon Lane, **Brentford,** is located in a Victorian waterworks and houses a unique collection of steam pumping engines, the largest of which is over three storeys high! Engines are operated at weekends only or by arrangement for schools. *Open daily (except Good Fri and Christmas) 11am-5pm, including Bank Hols.* 0181 568 4757 or send s.a.e. for 1999 events leaflet. (See Advert page x.)

Ⓒ Schools Open all year 🕯 ↔
Kew Gardens Gunnersbury

London Aquarium, County Hall, Riverside Building, Westminster Bridge Road, is the capital's first world-class aquarium featuring over 3000 specimens. See the fascinating and mysterious creatures from the globe's magnificent oceans, seas and rivers. Come face to face with piranhas from the tropics, poisonous lionfish from the Indian Ocean, find 2 metre long sharks or stroke a friendly ray in the Beach Pool. With informative and interesting daily talks programmes the London Aquarium is an educational and entertaining journey of discovery for all ages. *Open daily, 10am-6pm, (last admission 5pm).* 0171 967 8000. (See Advert page vi.)

Ⓔ Schools Open all year
↔ Westminster Waterloo

The London Butterfly House, Syon Park, **Brentford.** Many varied and colourful butterflies from all over the world are free to fly around as you walk through the large greenhouse. Lushly planted with flowering shrubs and tropical plants, it provides the right conditions for butterflies to fly, court, lay eggs, feed and bask in the sunlight. See some strange and wonderful looking caterpillars and a remarkable leaf-cutter ant colony! During the Summer, there is a section devoted to native British butterflies. A separate area displays spiders, scorpions and weird stick insects. *Open daily except Christmas, 10am-5pm, 3.30pm in Winter.* 0181 560 7272. www.butterflies.org.uk (See Advert page x.)

Ⓑ Schools Open all year
↔ Gunnersbury

London Transport Museum, Covent Garden Piazza, using imaginative and dynamic displays, takes you on a fascinating journey through time and recounts the story of the interaction between transport, the capital and its people from 1800 to the present day. Look out for the under 5s funbus, try the bus and tube simulators, meet characters from the past, see models and working displays and get interactive in the many "KidZones". More fun learning than you would have thought possible! Good educational material and lots of special holiday activities. *Open daily 10am-6pm, but 11am-6pm on Fridays. Closed 24-26th Dec.* 0171 836 8557 for recorded information. Education service: 0171 379 6344. www.ltmuseum.co.uk

Ⓒ Schools Open all year
↔ Covent Garden

Museum of the Moving Image, on the South Bank, close to Waterloo main line station, is an exciting and fascinating world of film, television and video to delight every member of the family. Discover some of the many secrets of film making and then have a go! Moving Magic Workshops frequently run in the school holidays where there are lots of drop-in activities organised for the family. *Open daily except 24th-26th Dec, 10am-6pm (last admission 5pm).* 0171 401 2636. (See Advert page x.)

Ⓓ Schools Open all year
↔ Waterloo

Price Codes for a family of four: Ⓐ: less than £5 Ⓑ: £5-£10 Ⓒ: £10-£15 Ⓓ: £15-£20 Ⓔ: £20-£30 Ⓖ:- Over £30 Ⓕ: Free
Schools: Range of educational opportunities available. 🕯 Birthday parties organised. ↔ Nearest tube station.

© Schools
Open all year
Q

The Museum of Rugby and the Twickenham Experience Tour, Rugby Road, **Twickenham,** a paradise for all enthusiasts, can be accessed by road, or by rail from Waterloo to Twickenham station. The home of English rugby has been impressively redeveloped and enlarged, incorporating the new and exciting multi-media Museum of Rugby. The history and growth of Rugby Union is charted using authentic mock-ups, interactive displays, archive film footage and unique objects. Also operating from the Museum are tours of the rugby stadium. You can walk alongside the hallowed turf, visit England's dressing room, walk through the players' tunnel and enjoy the magnificent views of the entire stadium from the top of the North Stand. *Open non-match days: Tues-Sat & Bank Hols 10.30am-5pm, Sun, 2-5pm. Match days: open for match ticket holders only. Closed Mon, 24th-26th Dec and Good Fri.* Tel: 0181 892 8877. (See Advert page vi.)

© Schools
Open all year

The Natural History Museum, Cromwell Road, sited in a most magnificent building, houses an amazing world of natural treasures and provides an opportunity to explore the Earth and its life, both past and present. See real dinosaur skeletons and life-sized robotic models in "Dinosaurs", marvel at the miracle of human life in "Human biology" and find out what an earthquake might feel like or what happens when a volcano erupts in "The Power within". Major new exhibitions, "From the beginning" and "Earth's treasury" offer chances to trace Earth's dramatic history from the 'big bang' to its inevitable death and to see a stunning array of gem and mineral riches, both beautiful and useful, that we take from the Earth. Discover, in newly-opened "Earth today and tomorrow", how science helps industry extract Earth's precious resources in a responsible and sustainable way. "Earth lab" offers those with an even keener interest, opportunities to discuss their 'finds' with scientists and explainers. Opening in mid July, a major new special exhibition "Voyages of discovery" will display for the first time some of the rarest and most precious items collected during some of history's most famous voyages of exploration. Focussing on the voyages of Sloane, Cook and Darwin, the exhibition will show how dangerous journeys, full of triumph and tragedy, revealed a world of huge diversity and richness which radically changed our ideas about life on Earth. *Open Mon-Sat, 10am-5.50pm, Sun, 11am-5.50pm. Closed 23rd-26th Dec.* 0171 938 9123. www.nhm.ac.uk (See Advert page viii.)

↔ South Kensington

Open all year

Pepsi IMAX 3D Theatre, The Pepsi Trocadero, Piccadilly Circus, offers movies for the millenium, where you don't just go to the movies, you are part of them! You can view 3D movies through special electronic headsets and become immersed deep into the action of the film. It is an amazing experience; striking 3D images will excite your senses and surround-sound will come from all directions. Premiere shows include the 3D sensation: "T-Rex Back to the Cretaceous" (PG), and "L5 - First City in Space" in 3D (U) and "Everest" (U) narrated by Liam Neeson. Call the ticket hotline: 0171 494 4143 for more information and prices. (See Advert page viii.)

↔ Piccadilly Circus

Let's Eat

Open all year

The Rainforest Cafe, 20 Shaftesbury Avenue, Piccadilly Circus, brings the sights, sounds and smells of a tropical rainforest into a 340-seat restaurant spanning three floors. Tour guides lead adventurers to their tables and orders are taken by experienced Safari guides. A range of tasty sounding foods are on offer with wonderfully exciting names and whilst choosing from the exotic menu, enjoy the special effects which include tropical rain showers, thunder and lightning storms, cascading waterfalls, rainforest mists and the cacophany of wildlife noises. Look out for the resident parrots, the myriads of tropical fish, the chattering gorillas, trumpeting elephants, slithering boa and life-sized crocodile! The resident curator runs on-site education programmes and will visit local schools with a parrot to talk about conservation and rainforests. *Party bookings are available for 6 or more Mon-Thurs anytime, before 6.30pm Fri and after 8pm on Suns. Open 12 noon-11pm, Sun-Thurs; 12 noon-12 midnight, Fri; 11.30am-12 midnight, Sat.* 0171 434 3111. www.rainforestcafe.uk.com. (See Advert page xii.)

↔ Piccadilly Circus

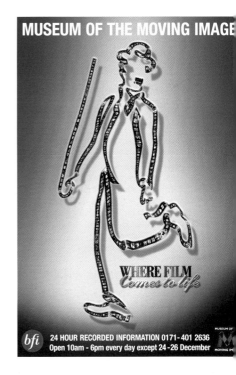

A PURRFECT DAY OUT
EDUCATIONAL INSPIRATION FOR CHILDREN!

SPECIAL SCHOOL PARTY RATES
£12.50 TUESDAY MATINEE
SUBJECT TO AVAILABILITY

TEACHERS' RESOURCE PACK
AVAILABLE ON REQUEST (ONE PACK PER SCHOOL)

PURRFECT DAY OUT
BACKSTAGE TOUR, LUNCH AT THEATRE AND SEE SHOW
£17.50 TUESDAY MATINEE
(MINIMUM 10 PEOPLE)

TAILOR-MADE WORKSHOPS
BY ARRANGEMENT

ONE CALL DOES IT ALL!

FOR FURTHER INFORMATION AND BOOKINGS PLEASE CONTACT JOHN SCARBOROUGH IN THE EDUCATION OFFICE
NEW LONDON THEATRE
TELEPHONE: 0171 400 5005 · GROUP BOOKINGS: 0171 400 5007 · E-mail: CATSUK@csi.com · www.reallyuseful.com

CLASSWORK AROUND THE STAGE

Rainforest Cafe

A WILD PLACE TO SHOP AND EAT

FEAST FROM OUR GENEROUS AND EXOTIC MENU

WONDER AT THE SIGHTS, SOUNDS AND SMELLS OF THE RAINFOREST

LEARN ABOUT VANISHING HABITATS AND THE ENVIRONMENT FROM OUR RESIDENT CURATOR

HELP SUPPORT OUR SCHOOLS' EDUCATIONAL PROGRAMME

SHAFTESBURY AVENUE, PICCADILLY CIRCUS

12 NOON TO 12 MIDNIGHT
(11PM SUNDAY - THURSDAY)

TEL: 0171 434 3111 FAX: 0171 434 3222
www.rainforestcafe.uk.com

A WILD PLACE TO SHOP AND EAT A WILD PLACE TO SHOP AND EAT A WILD PLACE TO SHOP AND EAT A WILD PLACE TO SHOP AND EAT

travel
through
time

by Sail and Rail

With a Sail and Rail ticket you can experience 1,000 years in a day. View London's riverside attractions from two different points - the sweep of DLR's elevated track and leisurely pace of a Thames riverboat. There's no better way to enjoy the stunning modern architecture and historic wharves of Docklands. Why not stop at one of the stations on the DLR route to visit the 800 ft. Canary Wharf Tower or the glories of Greenwich? Or just eat, drink and explore Docklands' unique surroundings.

ets are available from Westminster and Greenwich Piers, and Tower Gateway and Island Gardens Information Centres. Alternatively Travelcards are valid on DLR and single tickets are available from the boat operator.

For further information contact DLR Customer Services
on 0171 363 9700 or visit our web site at www.dlr.co.uk.

DOCKLANDS
LIGHT RAIL ®

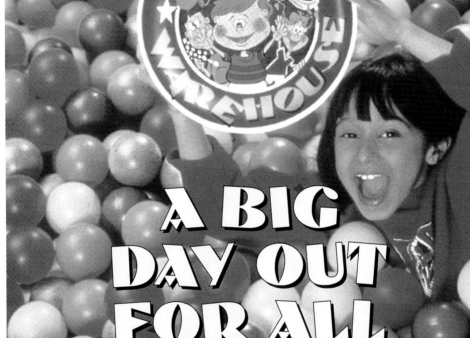

A BIG
DAY OUT
FOR ALL
THE FAMILY

BETTER PUBS. NO MYSTERY.

PUBS FOR THE FAMILY

Quite a range here from the more traditional, often country, pubs with indoor and/or outdoor facilities for children and the well organised, more standard pub/restaurants, some of which have large indoor play centres for which a charge is made. Many are open all day, some are supervised and welcome birthday party and other groups.

A4 ᐱ᠘ 🏚 **Cleeve, The Lord Nelson,** 01934 832170. On the A370 N of Congresbury. There are games and Billy Bear's Fun Fair.

ᐱ᠘ **Congresbury, Ship & Castle,** 01934 832794. Traditional pub with family area inside and large garden.

🎈 ᐱ᠘ 🏚 **Kewstoke, Old Manor,** 01934 515143. Situated on the Queensway Estate, the garden has an enclosed play area and inside is a "Charlie Chalk Fun Factory".

A5 ᐱ᠘ 🏚 **Bleadon, Hobbs Boat,** 01934 812782. On the main Bridgewater Rd. "Charlie Chalk Play Zone" and large garden.

🎈 🏚 **Glastonbury, The Tor Freehouse,** Street Rd, 01458 832393. Traditional pub with family room and bouncy castle.

B2 ᐱ᠘ **Littledean, The Belfry,** 01594 827858. On the edge of the Forest of Dean. Traditional pub with small fenced garden.

B3 ᐱ᠘ **Dursley, The George,** 01453 890270. On the A38. Traditional pub with garden, playground, aviary and enclosure with rabbits. BBQs in Summer.

B4 ᐱ᠘ **Bathford, The Crown,** 01225 852297. Just off A4 on A363 to Bradford-on-Avon. Friendly pub with family room. Magician on Sundays.

ᐱ᠘ **Bristol, The Merchants Arms,** Bell Hill, 0117 9518771. "Hungry Horse" restaurant with children's menu.

ᐱ᠘ **Travellers Rest,** Gloucester Rd, Patchway. 01454 612238. "Hungry Horse" restaurant with children's menu.

🎈 ᐱ᠘ 🏚 **Wessex Flyer,** Hengrove, 01275 834340. "Charlie Chalk Fun Factory", family restaurant and children's menu.

🎈 ᐱ᠘ 🏚 **Compton Martin, Ring o' Bells,** 01761 221284. Old country pub in Chew Valley with family room containing toys.

🎈 ᐱ᠘ 🏚 **Hanham, The Millhouse,** 178 High Street, 0117 9618836. An old millhouse with "Pirate Pete's Playden".

🎈 ᐱ᠘ 🏚 **Keynsham, Brass Mills,** near Bristol, 0117 9867280. "Charlie Chalk Play Zone", family dining area.

ᐱ᠘ **Nibley, The Swan,** 01454 312290. Traditional country pub outside Bristol, near Yate.

🎈 ᐱ᠘ **Westbury-on-Trym, The Beehive,** 0117 9623250. Large garden. Family area inside and children's menu.

🎈 ᐱ᠘ 🏚 **Yate, Brimsham Park,** 01454 315895. Family dining area, "Charlie Chalk Play Zone" and outdoor fenced area.

🎈 ᐱ᠘ 🏚 **The Lawns Inn,** Church Rd, 01454 314367. This attractive pub has an indoor play area separate to the main pub and a fenced playground outside.

Map Ref: Please refer to map on page 2.
ᐱ᠘ Outdoor play equipment.   🏚 Indoor play centre   🎈 Birthday parties

C2 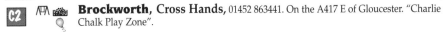 **Brockworth, Cross Hands,** 01452 863441. On the A417 E of Gloucester. "Charlie Chalk Play Zone".

Cheltenham, Seven Springs, Coberley, 01242 870219. "Hungry Horse" restaurant, children's menu.

Crickley Hill, Air Balloon, 01452 862541. On the edge of the Cotswold escarpment with lovely views, large enclosed garden.

Gretton, The Royal Oak, near Winchcombe, 01242 602477. Lovely pub with steam trains passing in Summer, tennis court.

Hucclecote, The Wagon and Horses, 87 Hucclecote Rd, 01452 616142. "Wacky Warehouse" play area, family dining and children's menu. (See Advert page 36.)

Quedgeley, The Salmon's Leap, Bristol Rd, 01452 721945. "Wacky Warehouse" play area, family dining and children's menu. (See Advert page 36.)

Tewkesbury, The Canterbury Inn, Ashchurch Rd, 01684 273098. Family room with games.

C3 **Kingscote, Hunter's Hall,** 01453 860393. On the road between Tetbury and Dursley, this friendly pub has a large garden.

Malmesbury, The Rose & Crown, Brokenborough, 01666 822302. Country pub with garden.

C4 **Chippenham, Cepen Park,** 01249 462096. "Charlie Chalk Play Zone", family dining and children's menu.

The Millhouse, Bath Rd, 01249 446474. An old millhouse with "Pirate Pete's Playden".

C5 **Trowbridge, Longs Arms,** Yarnbrook, 01225 753569. "Hungry Horse" restaurant with children's menu.

Standerwick, The Bell, 01373 830413. On the A36 NW of Warminster. Garden with tyre swings and wooden climbing unit.

Marston Meysey, Old Spotted Cow, 01285 810264. Large garden.

D3 **Swindon, The Friary,** Elstree Way, Abbey Meads, 01793 702081. "Wacky Warehouse" play area, family dining and children's menu. (See Advert page 36.)

The Running Horse, 01793 523903. Family dining, children's menu and enclosed outdoor play area.

Spotted Cow, Coate, 01793 485832. "Hungry Horse" restaurant with children's menu.

Sun Inn, Coate, 01793 523292. Family room and large garden with enclosed play area.

D4 **Chiseldon, The Patriots Arms,** near Swindon, 01793 740331. Handy stop from M4 (Jn 15). Family room and children's menu.

Wroughton, The Wroughton, High Street, 01793 812248. Fenced in garden with bouncy castle.

Map Ref: Please refer to map on page 2.
Outdoor play equipment.　Indoor play centre　Birthday parties

HISTORIC SITES, CASTLES, MUSEUMS & SCIENCE CENTRES

Step back in time and find out about days gone by, or step into the future and imagine yourself in the next century. Art, history, science and technology find a place here.

MAP REFS	PRICE CODES

A4

(B) **Helicopter Museum,** Locking Moor Road, **Weston-super-Mare.** The
Schools world's largest helicopter museum with over 70 helicopters and autogyros, including
Open all year a Russian Hind attack helicopter and Lynx world speed record holder. Models and
supporting displays located both indoors and out. Pleasure flights, picnic area. *Open
Cockpit Days every month and other special events during the Summer. Opening times vary.*
01934 635227.

(A) **Heritage Centre,** Wadham Street, **Weston-super-Mare.** A short walk from the
Schools town centre, discover the story of Weston, the sea and the countryside, in models and
Open all year pictures. Guided tours of the district and talks for schools, by arrangement. *Open
Mon-Sat, 10am-5pm. Closed 25th-26th Dec.* 01934 412144.

(B) **The Time Machine,** Burlington Street, **Weston-super-Mare.** Visit Clara's
Schools Victorian cottage – 3 rooms as they would have been at the turn of the century. Local
Open all year archaeology, geology and natural history displays. Art gallery and cafe. *Open daily,
Mar-Oct, 10am-5pm, Nov-Feb, 10am-4pm. Closed 25th-26th Dec, 1st Jan.* Ring for details
of special events and exhibitions. 01934 621028. Tickets reusable in same financial
year.

A5

(B) **The Cheddar Gorge Cheese Co.,** The Cliffs, **Cheddar.** Watch traditional
cheesemakers produce by hand the only 'real' Cheddar Cheese made in Cheddar
Gorge. Listen as they guide you through the process, visit the display of vintage dairy
memorabilia and sample the cheeses. See demonstrations by lacemakers and candle
carvers, have a go at 'throwing' a pot in the pottery and see the ancient art of cider
jar making. The Potting Shed welcomes gardeners and stocks local plants, flowers
and gifts. Taste the many varieties of fudge in the Fudge Kitchen. There is a
Conservatory Restaurant overlooking the village pond and stocks. *Open daily, Easter-
31st Oct, 10am-4pm.* 01934 742810. (See Advert outside back cover.)

(D) **Cheddar Showcaves,** Cheddar Gorge. Two beautiful caves set beneath
Schools dramatic limestone cliffs. There is a "Crystal Quest" underground adventure fantasy
Open all year and exhibition of life in the caves 9000 years ago. *Open May-mid Sept, 10am-5pm, mid
Sept-Apr, 10.30am-4.30pm. Closed 24th-25th Dec.* 01934 742343.

(A) **Glastonbury Tribunal Museum,** High Street. Part of a well
Schools preserved mediaeval building, this museum has items excavated from the Iron Age
Open all year Lake Villages. *Open daily, Apr-Sept, 10am-5pm, Oct-Mar, 10am-4pm.* Groups by
arrangement. 01458 832949.

(F) **King John's Hunting Lodge,** The Square, **Axbridge.** See "Free Places"
chapter.

B2

(C) **Clearwell Caves,** Coleford. See the miners' pick marks and the effects of fire
Schools setting on the walls in this extensive natural cave system which was mined for its iron
ore. Old mining equipment and vintage engines are also on display. Wrap up warm
and wear good shoes. Deep level and mid level trips can be organised. *Open beg Mar-
end Oct, 10am-5pm, Christmas Fantasy end Nov-Christmas.* Under 5s (F). 01594 832535.

Map Ref: Please refer to map on page 2.
Price Codes for a family of four: (A): less than £5 (B): £5-£10 (C): £10-£15 (D): £15-£20 (E): £20-£30 (G):- Over £30 (F): Free
Schools: Range of educational opportunities available. ● Birthday parties organised.

39

BERKELEY CASTLE

Just off the A38 between Bristol and Gloucester England's oldest inhabited castle and most historic home. Since 1153 twenty four generations of Berkeleys have transformed a savage Norman fortress into a truly stately home full of treasures and history.

The Castle is surrounded by sweeping lawns and Elizabethan terraced gardens. The Butterfly Farm is a tranquil oasis with hundreds of exotic butterflies in free flight.

There is a plant centre at the Butterfly Farm stocked with outdoor plants, shrubs, house plants, china and earthenware.

Free Car Park. Picnic Lawn, Tea Rooms. Gift Shop.

1999 Opening Times

April & May	**Tuesday to Sunday**	**1pm-5pm**
June	**Tuesday to Saturday**	**11am-5pm**
	Sunday	**1pm-5pm**
July & August	**Monday to Saturday**	**11am-5pm**
	Sunday	**1pm-5pm**
September	**Tuesday to Saturday**	**11am-5pm**
	Sunday	**1pm-5pm**
October	**Sundays Only**	**1pm-4.30pm**
Bank Holiday Mondays		**11am-5pm**

Enquiries: **01453 810332**

BERKELEY CASTLE

GLOUCESTERSHIRE GL13 9BQ TELEPHONE: 01453 810332

B2

Ⓑ **Dean Heritage Centre,** Camp Mill, Soudley, near **Cinderford.** Discover the
Schools story of the unique Forest of Dean landscape and its people, from prehistoric times to
Open all year the present day. Museum displays, Victorian cottage, millpond, nature cabin,
demonstration charcoal stack, woodland walks, adventure playground, craft shops,
cafe, picnic and BBQ facilities. *Open Feb, Mar & Oct, 10am-5pm, Apr-Sept, 10am-6pm,
Nov-Jan, Sat & Sun only, 10am-4pm. Closed 24th-26th Dec.* 01594 822170.

Ⓒ **Shambles Museum,** Church Street, **Newent.** Step out of 1990s Newent into
Schools a small Victorian country town. Enter the draper's house or enjoy gazing into the
windows of the bookseller and taxidermist. Something of interest around every
corner in this well organised museum. Picnic area. *Open Mar-Dec, Tues-Sun, 10am-
5pm, or dusk if earlier. Also open Bank Hols.* 01531 822144.

B3

Ⓒ **Berkeley Castle,** Berkeley. Midway between Bristol and Gloucester, just off
Schools the A38, England's oldest inhabited castle is well worth a visit. Surrounded by
sweeping lawns and Elizabethan terraced gardens, this fortress by the Severn Estuary
was completed by Lord Maurice Berkeley at the command of Henry II in 1153. The
family have not only preserved this ancient Castle, but gradually transformed a
savage Norman fortress into a truly stately home. You may wander through the
Castle at leisure or enjoy the free facility of a one-hour guided tour with an
experienced guide. Highlights are the massive Norman Keep with the Dungeon and
cell where King Edward II was murdered in 1327, Dining Room, Buttery, Kitchen and
impressive Great Hall. Picture what life in a castle would have been like. Before or
after your visit to the Castle, there is a small **Butterfly Farm** (see "Nature" chapter)
adjacent to the car park. *Open Apr-May: Tues-Sun 1-5pm, Jun & Sept: Tues-Sat 11am-
5pm, Sun 1-5pm, Jul & Aug: Mon-Sat 11am-5pm, Sun 1-5pm, Oct: Sun only 1-5pm, all bank
Hol Mons 11am-5pm.* 01453 810332 (See Advert page 40.)

Ⓐ **Jenner Museum,** Berkeley. This interesting museum is housed in Dr. Edward
Schools Jenner's beautiful Georgian home. Find out what he discovered about hedgehogs,
cuckoos and bird migration. Learn how his crucial experiment in 1796 (involving a
cow, a milkmaid and a small boy) has now led to the elimination of smallpox. *Open
Apr-Sept, Tues-Sat, 12.30-5.30pm, Sun, 1-5.30pm, Oct, Sun, 1-5.30pm.* 01453 810631.

Ⓕ Schools **Oldbury Power Station,** Oldbury-on-Severn. See "Free Places" chapter.

Ⓑ **Woodchester Mansion,** near **Nympsfield.** Hidden away in a secret valley,
Schools between Dursley and Stroud, this beautiful mansion was started in 1856 but
abandoned before completion. See how a vaulted ceiling is constructed, and
unfinished walls show the stages of plastering with lime. The Grand Stair with its
stained glass window, is now complete. *Phone for Open Day information, Easter-Oct.*
01453 860531.

B4

Ⓓ **American Museum,** Claverton Manor, **Bath.** A series of completely furnished
Schools rooms showing how the Americans lived from the 17th to 19th centuries. See how the
West was won and look out for the Indian tepee, pullman car and covered wagon.
Find out why Americans drive on the right! *Open 20th Mar-7th Nov, Tues-Sun, 2-5pm,
also Bank Hol Sun and Mons, 11am-5pm.* 01225 460503.

Ⓒ **Avon Valley Railway,** Bitton. See restored steam engines and take part in
Open all year special events throughout the year. 0117 9327296. (See also "Trips" chapter and
Advert page 6.)

Ⓒ **Bath Industrial Heritage Centre,** Julian Road, **Bath.** Enter the world
Schools of Victorian entrepreneur Mr. Bowler, whose business interests included an
Open all year engineering works and a soda water business. Also view displays of local industry
and work. *Open Easter-Oct, daily, 10am-5pm, Nov-Easter, Sat & Sun, 10am-5pm.* 01225
318348.

Map Ref: Please refer to map on page 2.
Price Codes for a family of four: Ⓐ: less than £5 Ⓑ: £5-£10 Ⓒ: £10-£15 Ⓓ: £15-£20 Ⓔ: £20-£30 Ⓖ:- Over £30 Ⓕ: Free
Schools: Range of educational opportunities available. Birthday parties organised.

Ⓑ Schools
Open all year
Bath Postal Museum, 8 Broad Street, is housed in the 19th century post office from which the world's first postage stamp was sent and displays the history of written communication from 2000 BC. Video room and children's activity room. Museum quiz sheets available. *Open daily, Mon-Sat 11am-5pm, Sun 2-5pm. Closed 25th-26th Dec and 1st Jan.* 01225 460333.

Ⓕ Schools
Open all year
Blaise Castle House Museum, Henbury, **Bristol.** See "Free Places" chapter.

Ⓑ
Schools
Building of Bath Museum, The Vineyards, The Paragon, **Bath,** shows how this city was built. Models include one of the entire city with push button illumination. Investigate life in Georgian Bath at the new touch screen computer. *Open Tues-Sun and Bank Hol Mons, 10.30am-5pm. Closed 1st Dec-mid Feb.* Groups by arrangement. 01225 333895.

Ⓐ
Schools
Open all year
City Museum and Art Gallery, Queens Road, **Bristol.** Find everything from sea-dragons, the original Bristol Boxkite and Egyptian tombs to mammals and shells of the south-west and wonderful archaeological and mineral displays, in this friendly well laid out museum. Special Events and Fun Days for children throughout the year. *Open daily, 10am-5pm.* 0117 922 3571. Under 16s Ⓕ.

Ⓑ
Open all year
Clifton Observatory and Caves, Bristol. The Observatory on the city side of the bridge houses a "camera obscura" installed in 1829. A rotating mirror in the roof reflects the panorama outside down onto a dish-shaped screen, weather permitting. Steps lead from inside the Observatory down a long, narrow descent to a viewing platform on the side of the cliff. *Open Mon-Fri, 11.30am-5pm, Sat and Sun, 10.30am-5pm. Closed Christmas.* 0117 9741242.

Ⓐ
Schools
Clifton Suspension Bridge Visitor Centre. Exhibits tell the story of Brunel's famous bridge from the first designs to its eventual completion in 1864. Budding engineers can learn how a suspension bridge works with a children's interactive bridge. *Open Apr-Sept, every day 10am-5.30pm Oct-Mar 11am-4pm Mon-Fri (5pm Sat & Sun.).* 0117 9744664. (See Advert page 55.)

Ⓒ
Schools
Dyrham Park, near **Bath.** On the A46, 7 miles N of Bath, the house is approached through ancient parkland. Built around 1700, the rooms have changed little since they were furnished. The Park is ideal for picnics. *House open, 27th Mar-31st Oct, Fri-Tues, 12-5.30pm, last admission 5pm, or dusk if earlier. Park open all year, daily, 12-5.30pm, or dusk if earlier. Closed 25th Dec, last admission 5pm or dusk if earlier.* 0117 937 2501.

Ⓒ
Schools
🎈
The Exploratory, Bristol Old Station, Temple Meads, **Bristol,** is an inspiration to all visitors, children and adults, who have ever asked the question why? Dozens of hands-on experiments help to make this a fascinating place to have fun whilst learning about science; how things work and why things are the way they are. Launch a hot air balloon, take a trip around the galaxy in the StarDome (available most weekends and school holidays), or visit the Body Lab. There are live science shows every Sunday afternoon and special events throughout the year. Excellent school visit facilities. *Open daily, 10am-5pm. Closing Autumn 1999.* "Explore @ Bristol" will open Spring 2000. 0117 907 5000. (See Advert page 50.)

Ⓐ
Schools
Georgian House, 7 Great George Street, **Bristol.** In this Merchant's town house see what life would have been like in Bristol at the end of the 18th century "upstairs and downstairs". Don't miss the unusual cold water plunge bath, the Sedan chair and the 19th century "rocker washer". *Open Apr-31st Oct, Sat-Wed, 10am-5pm.* 0117 921 1362. Under 16s Ⓕ.

Map Ref: Please refer to map on page 2.
Price Codes for a family of four: **Ⓐ:** less than £5 **Ⓑ:** £5-£10 **Ⓒ:** £10-£15 **Ⓓ:** £15-£20 **Ⓔ:** £20-£30 **Ⓖ:**- Over £30 **Ⓕ:** Free
Schools: Range of educational opportunities available. 🎈 Birthday parties organised.

B4

⑧ Schools **Holburne Museum and Craft Study Centre,** Great Pulteney Street, Bath. A relatively small museum, based upon the personal collections of Sir William Holburne; everything from porcelain and glass to furniture and paintings. Craft events and quiz sheets. 01225 466669.

Ⓐ Schools Open all year **Industrial Museum,** Princes Wharf, Wapping Road, **Bristol.** Discover the origins of the expression "Shipshape and Bristol fashion" in this museum dedicated to the transport industries associated with Bristol. See a full-size mock-up of Concorde's flight deck. The harbour steam railway and steam tug operate on certain dates from Mar-Oct. *Open 31st Oct-1st Apr, Sat & Sun 10am-5pm, 1st Apr-31st Oct, Sat-Wed, 10am-5pm.* 0117 9251470. Under 16s Ⓕ.

Ⓒ Schools Open all year **Museum of Costume,** Assembly Rooms, Bennett Street, **Bath.** View the tableaux of dressed figures and have 400 years of fashion and social history brought vividly to life. Personal audio tours and regular guided tours. *Open Mon-Sat, 10am-5pm, Sun, 11am-5pm. Last admission half hour before closing. Closed 25th-26th Dec.* Reduced price if combined with visit to Roman Baths. 01225 477785.

⑧ Schools **Priston Mill,** near **Bath,** is 6 miles SW of Bath. The spectacular waterwheel that powers this ancient Corn Mill will fascinate all ages. There are play areas, a scenic trailer ride, refreshments and nature trail. *Open Easter, Bank Hol Suns and Bank Hol Mons, 11.30am-5pm, Aug: Thurs, 2.15-5pm.* Groups all year by appointment. 01225 423894.

Ⓓ Schools Open all year **Roman Baths and Pump Room,** Abbey Church Yard, **Bath.** Follow in the footsteps of the Romans and explore the only hot spring baths in Britain, largely unchanged since Roman times. Choose the time of your visit carefully as there are always many visitors here. Personal audio tours and regular guided tours. *Open daily, Apr-Sept, 9am-6pm, Aug, also open 8-10pm. Oct-Mar, daily, 9.30am-5pm. Last admission half hour before closing. Closed 25th-26th Dec.* Reduced price if combined with visit to Museum of Costume. 01225 477785.

Ⓓ Schools Open all year **SS Great Britain and the Matthew,** Great Western Dock, **Bristol.** Brunel's great ship, the SS Great Britain, was launched in Bristol in 1843. She was the forerunner to all great passenger liners. Serving first as a luxury transatlantic liner, she then carried emigrants to Australia and troops to the Crimean War and ultimately became a cargo ship. She was eventually left to lie in the Falklands Islands where her hull had been used for storage. In 1970, she was towed 9,000 miles back to Bristol, where she now stands in the Great Western Dockyard, where she was built. Restoration is well under way to recreate her original splendour. The Matthew is a replica of the ship in which John Cabot sailed across the Atlantic in 1497 to discover Newfoundland. The journey was re-enacted in 1997. After a triumphant tour of Newfoundland and the Eastern Seaboard, she wintered in Toronto before returning to Bristol in Sept 1998 and is now moored alongside the SS Great Britain. Also on site is the Maritime Heritage Centre and Bristol Blue Glass Blowing demonstrations. Coffee shop. *Open daily, 10am-5.30pm Summer and 10am-4.30pm Winter. Closed 24th & 25th Dec.* 0117 926 0680 (See Advert page 49.)

Ⓕ Schools Open all year **Victoria Art Gallery,** Bridge Street, **Bath.** See "Free Places" chapter.

B5

⑧ Schools **Chewton Cheese Dairy,** Chewton Mendip. A working dairy with *visits available daily from Easter-end Sept, except Thur and Sun. Best time for viewing, 11.30am-2pm.* Groups (min 20 people) at any time, by appointment. The surrounding wooded area has play equipment, picnic tables and unusual farm animals. 01761 241666.

⑧ Schools **Peat Moors Centre,** Shapwick Rd, **Westhay.** Follow the story of peat and its extraction since Roman times. Visit the Iron-Age roundhouses and try crossing the ancient trackways. Iron-Age craft demonstrations most weekends in the Summer. *Open 1st Apr-31st Oct, 10am-5pm.* 01458 860697.

Map Ref: Please refer to map on page 2.
Price Codes for a family of four: Ⓐ: less than £5 ⑧: £5-£10 Ⓒ: £10-£15 Ⓓ: £15-£20 Ⓔ: £20-£30 Ⓖ:- Over £30 Ⓕ: Free
Schools: Range of educational opportunities available. 🍴 Birthday parties organised.

43

The National Trust

Chedworth Roman Villa
Yanworth, Cheltenham
Tel: 01242 890256

One of the best exposed Romano-British villa sites in Britain. The site includes a water shrine, two bath houses and 4th century mosaics.

Open Mar-Nov, Tues-Sun & Bank Holiday Mons
10am-5pm (4pm in Winter)
Admission: Adult £3.40, Child £1.70
Family £8.50

Ⓐ **Radstock, Midsomer Norton & District Museum,** houses a
Schools   good selection of displays depicting Victorian life. This museum was formerly
located in Haydon and will reopen in the Market Hall, Radstock mid-Summer 1999.
Telephone for details. 01761 437722.

Ⓑ **Wells Museum,** 8 Cathedral Green, **Wells,** is a small museum housing local
Schools   archeology and cave finds. Also featuring a sea dragon, miniature doll's house and
Open all year   the largest collection of samplers in the South West. *Open 29th Mar-18th Jul daily,
10am-5.30pm, 19th Jul-19th Sept 10am-8pm, 20th Sept-31st Oct 10am-5.30pm, 1st Nov-
28th Mar Wed-Sun, 11am-4pm. Closed 24th & 25th Dec.* 01749 673477.

Ⓓ **Wookey Hole Caves,** near **Wells.** The legendary home of the infamous
Schools   "Witch of Wookey". Visit the working paper mill and see paper being made as it was
Open all year   in Shakespeare's day. Visitors can also try their hand at paper making themselves.
The "Magical Mirror Maze" is very popular. Special rates for groups, by
arrangement. *Open Summer, daily 10am-5pm, Winter, 10.30am-4.30pm. Closed 17th-25th
Dec.* 01749 672243.

Ⓕ Schools **Cheltenham Art Gallery and Museum,** Clarence Street. See "Free
Open all year Places" chapter.

Ⓐ **City Museum and Art Gallery,** Brunswick Road, **Gloucester.** Displays
Schools   of local wildlife and archaeology, as well as local crafts from Roman sculptures to
Open all year   Grandfather clocks. Art exhibitions and special displays throughout the year. *Open
Mon--Sat, 10am-5pm, Jul-Sept, Sun 10am-4pm.* 01452 524131.

Ⓐ **Folk Museum,** 99-103 Westgate Street, **Gloucester.** Take a step back in time as
Schools   you enter the timber-framed building and experience local commercial, agricultural
Open all year   and social life in previous centuries. Victorian school room and displays of toys. Quiz
sheets for children. *Open Mon-Sat, 10am-5pm, incl. Bank Hols, Jul-Sept, also Sun, 10am-
4pm.* 01452 526467.

Ⓐ **Gustav Holst Birthplace,** 4 Clarence Road, **Cheltenham.** Small specialist
Schools   museum housed in the Regency terrace house in which Holst was born. Enjoy the
Open all year   display of toys in the upstairs nursery. *Open Tues-Sat, 10am-4.20pm.* 01242 524846.

Ⓑ **Hailes Abbey,** EH, **Winchcombe,** off B4362. Set in wooded pastureland, these
Schools   are the ruins of a beautiful 13th century Cistercian abbey. The ground plan is clearly
revealed and there are cloister remains together with an interesting site museum
containing examples of high quality sculpture. Self guided audio trail available. *Open
22nd Mar-31st Oct, daily, 10am-6pm. 1st Nov-31st Mar, Weekends only 10am-4pm. Closed
24th-26th Dec and 1st Jan.* 01242 602398.

Ⓒ **National Waterways Museum,** Llanthony Warehouse, Gloucester
Schools   Docks, **Gloucester.** Witness the lives of the people who built and used the canals.
Open all year   With the help of audio visual displays steer a narrow boat and build a canal.
Narrowboats, barges and dredgers moored alongside. *Open daily, 10am-6pm, closes
5pm in Winter. Under 5s* Ⓕ. 01452 318054.

Ⓑ **Nature in Art,** **Twigworth,** 2 miles N of Gloucester on the A38, this unique
Schools   museum is dedicated exclusively to art inspired by nature. Outdoor animal
Open all year   sculptures, play area, gift shop and refreshments. Artist in residence Feb-Nov. *Open
Tues-Sun, 10am-5pm. Other times by arrangement.* 01452 731422.

Ⓕ **Odda's Chapel,** Deerhurst, near **Tewkesbury.** See "Free Places" chapter.
Open all year

Ⓐ **Pittville Pump Rooms Museum,** Pittville Park, **Cheltenham.** Housed in
Schools   the Pump Rooms overlooking Pittville Park, the museum's tableaux and display
Open all year   cases show the development of costume in parallel with the history of the town from

Map Ref: Please refer to map on page 2.
Price Codes for a family of four: Ⓐ: less than £5 Ⓑ: £5-£10 Ⓒ: £10-£15 Ⓓ: £15-£20 Ⓔ: £20-£30 Ⓖ:- Over £30 Ⓕ: Free
Schools: Range of educational opportunities available. 🔔 Birthday parties organised.

45

1760-1940. *Open Oct-Apr, Mon, Wed-Sun, 11am-4pm, May-Sept, 10am-4.30pm.* 01242 523852.

Robert Opie Collection - Museum of Advertising and Packaging,
Schools
Open all year
The Albert Warehouse, Gloucester Docks, **Gloucester.** From utilitarian packets and tins to the bright and eye-catching packages designed to appeal to today's children, see how packaging and advertising slogans have changed through ten decades of shopping. *Open Mar-Sept, daily, 10am-6pm, Oct-Feb, Tues-Sun, 10am-5pm. Open Bank Hol Mons.* 01452 302309.

Soldiers of Gloucestershire Museum,
Schools
Open all year
Custom House, The Docks, Gloucester. An award-winning museum, the sights and sounds of well-constructed audio and visual displays involve you in the life of the Glosters – from glory at Alexandria, through tragedy in Flanders, to dramatic escape at Dunkirk and suffering and heroism in Korea. *Open Dec-Mar, Tues-Sun, 10am-5pm and Bank Hol Mons, Apr-Nov, daily, 10am-5pm.* 01452 522682.

Sudeley Castle,
Schools
Winchcombe. Find Charles I's bed and Katherine Parr's prayer book along with many fine paintings in this historic castle. Extensive gardens and grounds, wildfowl sanctuary and large adventure playground centred around a fort. Picnic area. Venue for many different events throughout the Summer. *Open Apr-Oct, daily, grounds 10.30am-5.30pm, castle 11am-5pm.* 01242 602308.

Winchcombe Folk and Police Museum,
Schools
Old Town Hall, displays local life and the industries which have come and gone – tobacco, wool, silk and paper. Also police uniforms from around the world. Groups by arrangement. *Open Apr-end Oct, Mon-Sat, 10am-5pm.* 01242 602925.

Athelstan Museum,
Town Hall, Cross Hayes, **Malmesbury.** See "Free Places" chapter.

Cirencester Lock-up,
Open all year
Trinity Road. See "Free Places" chapter.

Corinium Museum,
Schools
Open all year
Park Street, **Cirencester.** Roast Hedgehog for dinner, underfloor central heating and beautiful mosaics – get a sense of what it would have been like to live in Roman Britain's second largest town. Further displays reveal the importance of the Cotswold wool trade and Cirencester's part in the Civil War. *Open Apr-end Oct, Mon-Sat, 10am-5pm, Sun 2-5pm; Nov-Mar, Tues-Sat, 10am-5pm, Sun 2-5pm.* 01285 655611.

Atwell-Wilson Motor Museum,
Schools
Open all year
Downside, Stockley Lane, **Calne.** Many famous names of motoring in this small collection of vintage and classic cars, still in use. There is also a grass play area with traditional equipment. *Open Apr-Oct, Sun-Thurs, 11am-5pm; Nov-Mar, 11am-4pm.* 01249 813119.

Bowood House and Gardens,
Schools
Calne. A magnificent 18th century house with elegant rooms containing a wonderful collection of family heirlooms, built up over 250 years. These include paintings, porcelain, silver and such treasures as Queen Victoria's wedding chair, Napoleon's death mask, Lord Byron's Albanian soldier's costume and much more. Interesting rooms include Robert Adam's famous Library, Dr. Joseph Priestley's Laboratory where he discovered oxygen gas in 1774 and the Chapel. The surrounding Pleasure Grounds have lots to interest children. Open daily, 27th Mar-31st Oct, 11am-6pm or dusk. 01249 812102. www.bowood-estate.co.uk (See also "Wildlife" chapter and Advert page 50.)

Ⓕ Schools **Bradford-on-Avon Museum,** Bridge Street. See "Free Places" chapter.

Map Ref: Please refer to map on page 2.
Price Codes for a family of four: **A:** less than £5 **B:** £5-£10 **C:** £10-£15 **D:** £15-£20 **E:** £20-£30 **G:**- Over £30 **F:** Free
Schools: Range of educational opportunities available. ● Birthday parties organised.

46

Devizes Museum, Long Street. Founded in 1853, this award winning
Schools museum houses collections of archaeology, natural history and art. There are
Open all year interesting dioramas showing the natural history of Wiltshire, its wildlife and
geology. *Open Mon-Sat, 10am-5pm, closed Bank Hols.* 01380 727369. Mons Ⓕ.

Ⓒ **Fox Talbot Museum of Photography,** Lacock, within this lovely
Schools National Trust village, displays lots about early photography. *Phone for opening times.*
01249 730459.

Ⓐ **Kennet & Avon Canal Museum,** The Wharf, **Devizes.** With the aid of
Schools interactive video displays, this award winning museum tells the story of the creation
and restoration of the 87.5 mile long canal which passes through 104 locks and over
a height of 137m. *Open mid Feb-18th Dec, daily Summer, 10am-5pm. Winter, 10am-4pm.*
01380 721279. Under 16s Ⓕ.

Ⓑ **Lackham Country Attractions,** Lacock, **Chippenham.** Learn about the
Schools countryside, past and present, in the Agricultural Museum or see the animal park
and unusual plants. There are quiet riverside walks, an adventure playground and
picnic area. Groups welcome by arrangement. *Open 13th & 14th Mar and 23rd May,*
10am-4pm. Ring for further opening dates. 01249 466800.

Ⓕ Schools **Yelde Hall Museum,** Market Place, **Chippenham.** See "Free Places" chapter.

Ⓑ **Farleigh Hungerford Castle** EH, is W of **Trowbridge** on the A366. These
Schools extensive ruins of a 14th century castle include a splendid chapel with wall
Open all year paintings, stained glass and the tomb of Sir Thomas Hungerford, builder of the
castle. *Open Apr-Oct, daily, 10am-6pm (5pm in Oct), Nov-Mar, Wed-Sun, 10am-4pm.*
01225 754026.

Ⓖ **Longleat House,** **Warminster,** is one of the finest Elizabethan Houses in
Schools Britain and is the family home of the Marquess and Marchioness of Bath. The house
Open all year is set in a beautiful valley, surrounded by lakes and parkland. There are magnificent
state rooms with superb paintings and furniture and a fascinating Victorian kitchen.
Lord Bath's own murals add to the interest, making this house well worth visiting.
Other attractions include a Safari Park *(open 13th Mar-31st Oct)*, balloon rides,
Postman Pat Village, Adventure Castle, Doctor Who Exhibition and much more.
Save money with a passport ticket to all attractions or pay as you go. *The house is open*
all year except 25th Dec, Easter-Sept, 10am-6pm. Rest of the year 10am-4pm. 01985 844400.
www.longleat.co.uk (See "Wildlife" chapter and Advert on page 50.)

Ⓕ Schools **Trowbridge Museum,** The Shires, Court Street. See "Free Places" chapter.
Open all year

Ⓑ **Chedworth Roman Villa,** NT, **Yanworth.** 8 miles SE of Cheltenham. These
Schools are the remains of one of the best exposed Romano-British villas in Britain. Today
you can see the ruins of this 1600 year old 'stately home' and imagine yourself back
in the 4th century. As you look at the surviving mosaics, the hypocausts (Roman
under floor central heating), water shrine and the many objects in the site museum,
you can get a flavour of life when Britain was part of the Roman Empire. There is an
audio tour and programme of Special Events throughout the year. *Open Mar-Nov,*
Tues-Sun and Bank Hol Mons, 10am-5pm (4pm in Winter). 01242 890256. (See Advert
page 44.)

Ⓐ **Cotswold Countryside Collection,** **Northleach.** The story of local rural
Schools life is housed in what remains of an 18th century prison. Hear judges pass sentence
and see where you would have been imprisoned. Displays of life on the farm and
colourful harvest wagons. *Open Apr-Oct, Mon-Sat, 10am-5pm, Sun, 2-5pm. Bank Hol*
Sun & Mon 10am-5pm, 1st Nov-18th Dec open Sat 10am-4pm. 01451 860715.

Historic Sites, Castles, Museums & Science Centres

Map Ref: Please refer to map on page 2.
Price Codes for a family of four: Ⓐ: less than £5 Ⓑ: £5-£10 Ⓒ: £10-£15 Ⓓ: £15-£20 Ⓔ: £20-£30 Ⓖ: Over £30 Ⓕ: Free
Schools: Range of educational opportunities available. 🔔 Birthday parties organised.

47

The Cotswolds Motor Museum and Toy Collection, Bourton-on-the-Water.
Ⓐ Schools
A fascinating collection of 30 vintage motor cars and motor cycles and one of the largest collections of vintage advertising signs, automobilia and toys. Don't miss television star "Brum" or the period gramophones! Quiz sheets for children. Ticket to Motor Museum also permits entry to Museum of Village Life in the adjoining mill. *Open beg Feb-end Nov, daily 10am-6pm.* 01451 821255.

The Dragonfly Maze, Rissington Rd, Bourton-on-the-Water.
Ⓑ Schools
Open all year
Find your way around this amazing rebus puzzle maze, solving clues as you wander through the quarter mile of twisting pathways. *Open Summer, daily, 10am-5.30pm, (telephone for Winter opening times).* 01451 822251.

Keith Harding's World of Mechanical Music, High Street, Northleach.
Ⓒ Schools
Open all year
Listen to the amazing self-playing musical instruments covering three centuries of entertainment in the home and see beautiful clocks, musical boxes and automata. *Open every day, except Christmas, 10am-6pm.* 01451 860181.

Miniature World, High St, Bourton-on-the-Water.
Ⓑ Schools
Step into the world of miniature and marvel at the time and patience that has gone into the 50 exhibits. *Open mid Apr-mid Oct, 10am-5.30pm.* 01451 810121.

Model Railway, Box Bush, High Street, Bourton-on-the-Water.
Ⓑ
Press buttons and bring the 00/H0 and N gauge railways to life. Enjoy the wonderful details of the background scenery. *Open Apr-Sept daily, 11am-5.30pm, Oct-Mar, Sat & Sun, 11am-5pm, limited opening in Jan.* 01451 820686.

Model Village, The Old New Inn, Bourton-on-the-Water.
Ⓑ Schools
Open all year
Find the model of the model of the model village, listen to the singing from the church in this 1/9th scale version of Bourton-on-the-Water originally opened on Coronation Day in 1937. *Open Summer, daily, 9am-6pm, Winter, daily, 10am-4pm. Closed 25th Dec.* 01451 820467.

Perfumery Exhibition, Bourton-on-the-Water.
Ⓑ Schools
Open all year
Learn about perfume in the "smellevision" cinema, stroll through the enchanting perfume garden or try your hand at the perfume quiz. More interesting for older children. *Open Mon-Sat, 9.30am-5pm, Sun, 10.30am-5pm. Closed 25th & 26th Dec.* 01451 820698.

Arlington Mill Museum, Bibury.
Ⓐ Schools
Open all year
Examine the efficiency of cogs, wheels and pulleys, or take a guided tour of working machinery, the herb garden and Victorian way of life. *Open daily, Summer, 10am-6pm, Winter, 10am-5pm. Closed 25th-26th Dec.* 01285 740368.

Great Western Railway Museum, Faringdon Road, Swindon.
Ⓑ Schools
Set in the heart of Brunel's railway village, the museum tells the history of Swindon in the age of the GWR. See the magnificently restored locomotives, step on to the footplate of a train cab and try on the 'Grease Top' for size. *Open Mon-Sat, 10am-5pm, Sun, 2-5pm. Last admission 4.30pm. Closing end Sept 1999. New Museum called "Steam" opening Spring 2000.* 01793 466555.

Lydiard House and Park, Lydiard Tregoze, near Swindon.
Ⓐ Schools
Open all year
Close to Jn16 on the M4. This beautiful park with walks and play areas (see "Free Places" chapter), surrounds an 18th century house where you will see fine furniture and family portraits of the St. John family. *House open Summer, Mon-Fri, 10am-1pm, 2-5pm, Sat 10am-5pm, Sun, 2-5.30pm; Winter, Mon-Sat, 10am-1pm, 2-4pm, Sun, 2-4pm.* 01793 770401.

Railway Village Museum, 34 Faringdon Road, Swindon.
Ⓑ Schools
Open all year
Step back in time in this restored railwayman's cottage with many original fittings. *Open Mon-Fri, 10am-1pm, 2-5pm, Sat, 10am-5pm, Sun 2-5pm.* Price included with ticket from GWR Museum. 01793 493189.

Swindon and Cricklade Railway, Blunsdon Station.
Ⓐ
Open all year
See restored steam engines and inside an old signal box. There is a museum and collectors' corner and rides up the track on steaming days. *Open every weekend.* (See "Trips" chapter.) 01793 771615.

Map Ref: Please refer to map on page 2.
Price Codes for a family of four: Ⓐ: less than £5 Ⓑ: £5-£10 Ⓒ: £10-£15 Ⓓ: £15-£20 Ⓔ: £20-£30 Ⓖ:- Over £30 Ⓕ: Free
Schools: Range of educational opportunities available. 🕭 Birthday parties organised.

MAP REFS

 PRICE CODES

Ⓕ Schools **Swindon Museum and Art Gallery,** Bath Road. See "Free Places"
Open all year chapter.

D4

Ⓐ **Alexander Keiller Museum,** Avebury. The life of Neolithic man in the
Schools area is illustrated in exciting displays. See tools, skeletons and a prehistoric child
Open all year called Charlie. *Open 1st Apr-31st Oct, daily, 10am-6pm; 1st Nov-31st Mar, daily, 10am-4pm. Closed 24th-26th Dec and 1st Jan.* 01672 539250. Educational groups by
arrangement. Ⓕ.

Ⓕ Schools **Avebury Stone Circle,** Avebury. See "Free Places" chapter.
Open all year

Ⓑ **Pumping Station** beside the Kennet and Avon Canal, **Crofton,** houses two
early beam engines. *Open Easter-Oct, daily, 10.30am-5pm.* 'Steam Days', ring for
details. 01672 870300.

Schools **Wroughton Airfield Science Museum,** Wroughton Airfield. This
collection of commercial aircraft, road transport, marine and agricultural items is
open to the public on special event days held through the Summer. Prices vary according to
event. Plenty of picnic areas. Groups by arrangement. Contact for programme. 01793
814466.

TWO TO SEA

Two of Bristol's most famous ships - the ss Great Britain and The Matthew, now lie side by side to form a combined maritime exhibition.

The ss Great Britain is the restored ship, built by Isambard Kingdom Brunel in 1843, and is not only the forerunner of all luxury passenger liners that followed, but also the only one to survive the first half of the 19th century.

The Matthew is a replica of John Cabots 15th century ship which sailed from Bristol to discover Newfoundland in 1497 (this journey was re-enacted in 1997).

• One ticket enables visitors to go aboard both ships and visit the Maritime Heritage Centre & Bristol Blue Glass • Guided tours by arrangement
• Audio visual introduction • Banquets/weddings • Coffee shop • Gift shop
• Car/coach parking, coaches welcome (limited facilities for the disabled)

ss GREAT BRITAIN. Great Western Dock, Gas Ferry Road, Bristol BS1 6TY   Tel: 0117 926 0680   Information line: 0117 929 1843   Fax: 0117 925 5788

50

PLACES TO GO OUTSIDE THE AREA

Visit some exciting places just a little further afield.

PRICE CODES

BERKSHIRE

LEGOLAND® Windsor, is a wonderful day out for all the family. From the "Beginning" the Park spreads out beneath you, set in beautifully landscaped parkland. Take the Hill Train down to the heart of the Park or stroll down and stop and marvel at Miniland on the way. 20 million LEGO bricks were used to create this area and it's amazing. The latest attraction to be added is Castleland, where you can board The Dragon, a roller-coaster ride which explores the Castle and then plunges through the trees outside. (Riders must be 1.1m tall). The LEGO Mindstorms Centre is an exciting new technology workshop which introduces children from the age of 9 to the world of robotics. The Wild Woods offer the chance to pan for gold, search for pirates, explore the Rat Trap and ride the Pirate Falls. Don't forget to visit the DUPLO Gardens for younger children, the Driving School, the Sky Rider, My Town and Brickadilly's Circus and Fairground. Good food, birthday packages, season tickets and an educational service are all on offer. *Open daily, 13th Mar-31st Oct, 10am-6pm or dusk if earlier. Summer School hols, 10am-8pm.* 0990 04 04 04. www.legoland.co.uk (See Advert inside back cover.)

(G)
Schools

OXFORDSHIRE

Cotswold Wildlife Park, Burford, occupies 160 acres of gardens and parkland with a wide variety of animals to be seen as you walk around. The wildlife varies from reptiles to tarantulas, penguins to rhinos as well as endangered Asiatic lions, Amur leopards and Red Pandas in large enclosures. Extensive picnic lawns, shaded by oaks and California Redwoods, also provide a setting for a large adventure playground and children's farmyard. A brass-rubbing centre and cafeteria are located in the listed Victorian Manor in the centre of the Park. During the Summer there are special events and a narrow-gauge railway runs from Apr-Oct. The Park encourages school parties and has all-round pushchair and wheelchair access. *Open daily at 10am. Last admissions Mar-Sept 5pm. Please check Winter closing times.* 01993 823006. (See Advert page 55.)

(D)
Schools
Open all year

The Water Fowl Sanctuary and Children's Farm, Wigginton Heath, off the A361 Banbury to Chipping Norton road, is a wonderful place to take children, whatever the weather, with new aviaries for 1999. Mix with the rabbits and feed the many birds and animals with grain on sale, or bring your own. There is a trail laid out to follow around with hundreds of birds and animals on view. Throughout the year there are many baby animals and birds for adults to pick up, and allow the children to sit and cuddle. Easy to read and interesting information tells you about many of the birds and animals including goats, sheep, ponies, cattle, pigs, ducks, swans, ostriches, emus and rheas from a bygone age. There is an adventure playground to enjoy. Covered picnic areas are available. Practical clothing and footwear, especially wellies, if wet, are recommended for a visit to this Conservation Award haven. School parties are very welcome with quizzes, National Curriculum worksheets. Half price for schools. Incubators/eggs available for schools. *Open daily, except Christmas Day, 10.30am-6pm, or dusk.* 01608 730252. Free parking, free pre-visit for teachers, 10 people 10% discount if pre-booked. www.visitbritain.com (See Advert page 55.)

(C)
Schools
Open all year

Price Codes for a family of four: **A**: less than £5 **B**: £5-£10 **C**: £10-£15 **D**: £15-£20 **E**: £25-£30 **G**:- Over £30 **F**: Free
Schools: Range of educational opportunities available. Birthday parties organised.

PRICE
CODES

SOUTH WALES

© **Techniquest,** Stuart Street, **Cardiff**, 10 mins from the M4 and 40 mins from the Severn
Schools Bridge. This leading science discovery centre in Cardiff Bay, is neither a museum nor
Open all year funfair, but contains elements of both. Adults and children can satisfy their curiosity and
experience science through 160 interactive exhibits, puzzles, challenges and scientific
marvels including a few live ones! Fly a hot air balloon, launch a hydrogen rocket or play
a harp without strings! The Discovery Room, where you can become a forensic detective or
investigate ultraviolet light, Planetarium and state of the art Science Theatre are special
features (subject to availability) for which there is a small extra charge. *Open daily, Mon-Fri,
9.30am-4.30pm, Sat, Sun and Bank Hols, 10.30am-5pm. Last admission 45 minutes before closing.
Closed for a short break at Christmas.* 01222 475 475. www.tquest.org.uk (See Advert inside
front cover.)

SOUTH WILTSHIRE

© **Farmer Giles Farmstead,** Teffont, is W of Salisbury, on the B3089 and just off
Schools the A303 London - Exeter Road, 12 miles W of Stonehenge. If you love the countryside, you
Open all year cannot fail to enjoy a visit to the Farmstead. Set in glorious Wiltshire downland, it is a real
working dairy farm where you can watch the cows being milked, bottle feed lambs and
feed other animals. There is an adventure playground with tractors to sap the energy of
active children. Take a relaxing walk along the picturesque Beech belt walk meeting
Highland, Longhorn and Dexter Cattle, Shetland ponies, donkeys, Wiltshire Horn, Badger
and Hebridean Sheep. Relax by the ponds with the windpump and waterfall and return to
pets corner, the large exhibition areas, gift shop and licensed restaurant with home cooked
food. It is a venue for all weathers, with outdoor and indoor picnic areas. Schools are
welcome by arrangement to use good educational facilities. *Open daily, 10am-6pm, 20th Mar-
7th Nov and Winter weekends.* 01722 716338. (See Advert page 55.)

SURREY

© **The Great Thorpe Park,** Staines Rd., **Chertsey**, located on the A320 between
Schools Staines and Chertsey, with easy access from Jns 11 & 13 off M25, is a marvellous family
leisure park spread over an attractive 500 acre site with a wide variety of excellent
attractions on offer. There are rides to suit all ages from the refreshing Tea Cup Ride, the
Flying Fish rollercoaster, the Dino Bumper Boat Ride, the Dare Devil Bumper Cars, the Wet!
Wet! Wet! Torpedo Water Slides, Loggers Leap, Depth Charge and Thunder River rides to
X:/No Way Out, the only backwards plummeting roller coaster ride, in total darkness, in
the world! To slow the adrenalin rate, take a boat or train to the Great Thorpe Farm, where
you can step back in time with the animals, relax on the Fantasy Reef beach, or wander
around Ranger Country for some jungle adventures and a swing on Mr Monkey's Banana
Boat Ride. There are many schemes for purchasing tickets by phone in advance, cost
reductions on "Plan-Ahead" tickets and a Parent and Toddler Pass. With so much to see
and do, you may have to visit again and again, and the new Harley Pass season ticket, valid
for a year from purchase, can give you a whole twelve months of excitement, well worth
the investment. Excellent educational material for school parties. *Open daily, Mar-Oct.* There
is always something special going on right up until the last day of the season! For full
opening details, phone the Information Hotline: 01932 562633. Plan-Ahead Line: 0990
880800. www.thorpepark.co.uk (See Advert pages 3 & 4.)

WARWICKSHIRE

© **The Shire Horse Centre,** Clifford Road, **Stratford-upon-Avon**. Located 2 miles S
Schools of town centre, just off the A3400. A great day out for children of all ages. Fun, excitement
Open all year and lots of animals, from shire horses to baby rabbits. Opening Easter 1999 is the Shire
Horse Theatre where you will learn about how these great horses once worked in the fields
and the jobs they did. From here, move on to experience the real Gentle Giants, with foals
usually born late April. There are many rare breeds of farm animals; pigs and their cheeky
piglets, cattle, friendly goats, woolly sheep (lambing January to Easter). Children will love
Pat-a-Pet, where they can hold various pets, including rabbits. The playground provides
excitement with its fantastic hyperslides (8m drop slide, wave slides and more), tractor
land, sandpit with diggers, scramble net and a tiny tots climb and slide. "Sammy Shires
Playbarn and Family Room" has indoor tunnels, slides and scramble net surrounded by
balls (extra charge). Special kids menu, highchairs available. *Open daily, Mar-Oct, 10am-5pm,
Sat-Wed, Nov-Feb.* 01789 266276.

Competition Page

WIN A RALEIGH BIKE!

Rearrange these letters into a well known sport

G L I C N C Y

☐ ☐ ☐ ☐ ☐ ☐ ☐

Enter one or all of the competitions below. Fill in your details overleaf and return this page to us by 31st October 1999.

Do you have a bike? ☐ Yes ☐ No

How often do you go family cycling?
☐ Rarely ☐ Sometimes ☐ Often

15 FAMILY TICKETS TO BE WON TO DISNEY'S BEAUTY AND THE BEAST

at The Dominion Theatre in London

Read the write up in the London section of this guide and tell us the Beauty's name _____

How many times a year do you visit the Theatre?
☐ 1 or less ☐ 2-3 ☐ More than 3

WIN ENTRANCE TO THORPE PARK

1st Prize A family Harley Pass season ticket

& then 15 family tickets (each for 4 persons)

Ring the odd one out

How many times have you visited Thorpe Park
☐ Never ☐ 1-3 times ☐ More than 3 times

How long is your journey time to Thorpe Park?
☐ Less than ½hr. ☐ ½hr-1½ hrs. ☐ more than 1½hrs.

Completed sheets will be entered in all three draws.
The winners will be the first correct entries drawn in each of the three draws.

Competition Reply

Must reach us by 31st October 1999

The winners will be the first correct entries drawn in each draw. Winners will be notified by post during November 1999. No responsibility can be accepted for entries lost, defaced or delayed in the post. No correspondence can be entered into and the decision of the publishing company is final

Name...

Address...

....

County......................................Postcode..

Age of Book Purchaser ☐ under 25 ☐ 25-35 ☐ 35-50 ☐ Over 50

Age of Children..

Book purchased from ☐ Bookshop ☐ Newsagents ☐ Garage

☐ Attraction ☐ Supermarket ☐ Tourist Information

Have you bought a Let's Go Guide before? ☐ Yes ☐ No

Please rate Let's Go Guide on a scale 1-5, 5=excellent ☐

& OTHER LET'S GO EDITIONS

ORDER FORM

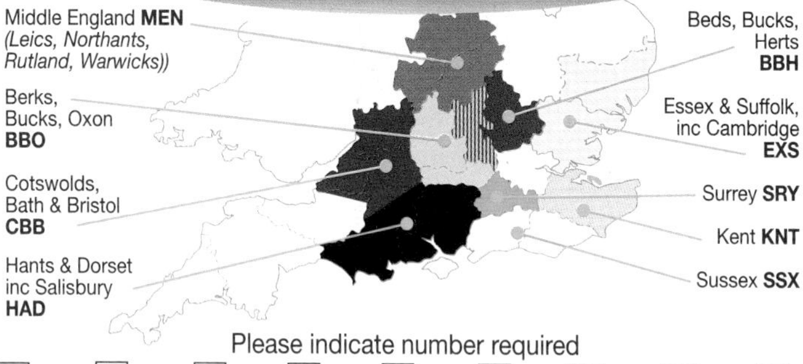

Middle England **MEN**
(Leics, Northants, Rutland, Warwicks))
Berks, Bucks, Oxon **BBO**
Cotswolds, Bath & Bristol **CBB**
Hants & Dorset inc Salisbury **HAD**
Beds, Bucks, Herts **BBH**
Essex & Suffolk, inc Cambridge **EXS**
Surrey **SRY**
Kent **KNT**
Sussex **SSX**

Please indicate number required

☐	☐	☐	☐	☐	☐	☐	☐	☐
BBH	BBO	CBB	EXS	HAD	KNT	MEN	SRY	SSX

I enclose a cheque made payable to Cube Publications for £ ☐

(Mail order price = £3.30 for EXS, MEN. £3.50 for all other editions

Use the form above to tell us your name and address

Please send to Cube Publications, Bank House, Mavins Road, Farnham, Surrey GU9 8JS

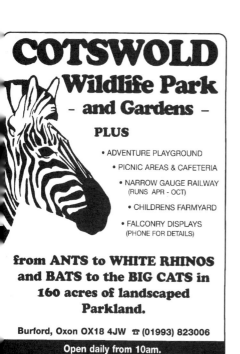

INDEX

CLIMBING
AND WALL PLANTS

ARTHUR HELLYER

HarperCollins*Publishers*

Products mentioned in this book

Benlate* + 'Activex'	contains	benomyl
'Nimrod'-T	contains	bupirimate/pirimicarb
'Roseclear'	contains	bupirimate/pirimicarb /triforine
'Rapid'	contains	pirimicarb
'Sybol'	contains	pirimiphos-methyl

Products marked thus *'Sybol'* are trade marks of Imperial Chemical Industries plc
Benlate * is a registered trade mark of Du Pont's
Read the label before you buy: use pesticides safely

Editors Maggie Daykin, Susanne Mitchell
Designer Chris Walker
Picture research Moira McIlroy

First published 1988 by
HarperCollins Publishers

This edition published 1992

© Marshall Cavendish Limited 1988, 1992

A CIP catalogue record for this book is available from the British Library.

Photoset by Bookworm Typesetting
Printed and bound in Hong Kong by Dai Nippon Printing Company

Front cover: Lonicera periclymenum 'Belgica'
Back cover: Wisteria floribunda macrobotrys
Both photographs by Michael Warren

CONTENTS

INTRODUCTION

Climbers are the 'drapes' of the garden. The functions performed indoors by wallpapers, curtains and coverings are taken over in the open by a great variety of climbing plants and some others that, though not really climbers, can be made to serve a similar purpose by proper pruning and training.

Parthenocissus tricuspidata 'Veitchii', the vigorous and self-clinging vine, seen here in the full glory of its autumnal colouring. The leaves are ovate or trifoliate in form; the fruits dark blue. Provides very dense wall-coverage.

Types of climber True climbers hold themselves aloft by a variety of means. The simplest, seen in climbing roses and the ornamental brambles, is to thrust themselves into shrubs and trees, finding support among the branches and perhaps gaining a little extra hold by means of thorns or prickles. A little more complicated are the twiners, which twist themselves around almost anything that is not too thick. In the wild, like the thrusters, they rely mainly on trees and shrubs for support and by this simple means some – such as the wisterias and climbing honeysuckles – can ascend to considerable heights.

Then there are the tendril climbers, for example, sweet peas, vines and clematis, which modify some of their stems or leaf stalks to coil around anything fairly slender that offers support. In gardens they are happy on trellis, wires or twiggy branches but they cannot cope with a large surface such as a post or thick pillar.

Finally, most ingenious of all, are the self-clingers which even cope with a wall without need for any aids. Some, like the ivies, do it with modified roots which get into the smallest crevices or irregularities and even succeed in holding on to completely smooth surfaces, though not quite so securely. Some of the plants popularly known as Virginia creeper cling with little adhesive pads formed on the ends of tendrils but other Virginia creepers have tendrils without the pads and so need something around which to twist. It is such duplications in the use of popular names that make it essential sometimes to use botanical names – they are more precise. The self-clinging Virginia creeper is *Parthenocissus tricuspidata*, a name that belongs to no other plant.

6

Some plants treated as climbers have no natural aptitude for climbing; they are really shrubs but with pruning and training can be spread out on walls, along fences or on screens. Many of the shrubs pressed into service as climbers are evergreens, that is, they retain their leaves all winter. Not a great many true climbers do this and are also hardy enough to be grown outdoors in Britain and there are many situations in which it is an advantage to have a covering that remains equally leafy throughout the year.

There are also some true climbers that are herbaceous, that is, they die down in winter and grow up again the following spring. Some twine, some cling by their tendrils and all can be very useful when permanent cover is not required. The most popular fully herbaceous kinds are *Lathyrus grandiflorus*, the Everlasting Pea, *Humulus lupulus* 'Aureus', the Golden Hop and *Tropaeolum speciosum*, the Flame Flower.

Eccremocarpus scaber is a semi-woody climber which out of doors in Britain is usually 'killed' to ground level each winter but in sunny, sheltered places often starts to grow again the following spring so that it really behaves like a herbaceous perennial. According to their local climate, gardeners treat this popular climber as a half-hardy annual, a half-hardy biennial, a herbaceous plant or a shrubby climber. Whatever the system of management, it is always increased by seed.

There are also a number of genuine, annual climbers which can be very useful for quick cover. I have devoted a short section to these (and biennials) as they require special treatment (see pages 14–15).

ABOVE Hederas are good companion plants for vines. Here, the cream and green of *Hedera helix* 'Jubilee' complements the purple foliage of *Vitis vinifera purpurea* and will still clothe the wall when the vine takes its winter rest.

RIGHT Roses and clematis are another popular combination. And both plants will usually oblige with a second flowering if conditions are right.

PLANTING CLIMBERS

Without exception, all of the plants included in this book will grow in any reasonably fertile soil. It does not have to be specially acid or alkaline, it need not be very rich but it does need to be reasonably supplied with plant food. It should also be well dug or forked before the climbers are planted so that the young roots can penetrate it easily. Later on, as they become established, the roots will be able to find their way almost anywhere but at the outset they need assistance.

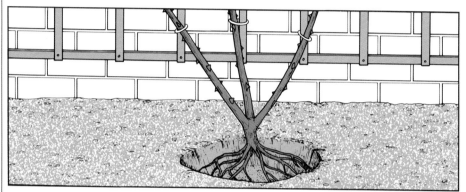

Soil preparation One of the hazards with climbers used to cover walls is that the soil close to a wall is almost always a lot drier than the soil right out in the open. For this reason it is not wise to plant very close to a wall, though this might seem the neatest way of going about it. Some 30–45cm (1–1½ft) away the soil will get more direct rainfall and it will still be possible to bring the stems back to the wall. An area at least 45cm (1½ft) square and as much deep should be prepared for each plant, not just by breaking it up with spade or fork but also by mixing in some manure (it can be the specially prepared bagged type), 'Forest Bark' Ground and Composted Bark, or peat plus a little fertilizer. If the ground is hard or sticky it may be better to remove it altogether from the planting sites and replace with better soil from another part of the garden or from a garden centre.

Roses Climbing plants are almost always supplied by nurserymen well established in containers from which they can be transplanted at any time of the year. An exception may be climbing roses, especially if purchased from a rose specialist. Then delivery is likely to be in the autumn or winter and the plants will have been lifted from the open ground. There will be no soil on the roots, so they must either be re-planted immediately where they are to grow or have their roots well covered with soil to keep them moist until it is convenient to plant them permanently.

There is nothing wrong with bare root planting provided it is done well and promptly while the plants are leafless. Advantages are that the plants will probably have a more outward searching root system and that a greater selection of varieties may be available.

8

Other plants In general, plants lifted from the open ground will require wider planting holes than those removed from containers since the roots of the former should be spread out in a natural way. When planting in autumn and winter it may be wise also to loosen the outer roots of container plants and lead them out into the surrounding soil but it is unwise to cause root disturbance when planting in summer.

With all planting the aim should be to cover the uppermost roots with from 2.5–5cm (1–2in) of soil. Deep planting will retard growth; shallow planting may allow some roots to dry out and be killed. With container plants, a safe rule is to cover the ball of soil with 2.5cm (1in) of the new soil. With bare root plants the old soil mark can usually be seen on the stems and this should also be buried to a depth of 2.5cm (1in).

Unless the soil is very wet, water after planting giving at least a gallon per plant to settle the soil in around the roots. When planting in spring or summer, frequent repeat waterings are likely to be necessary until the plants are growing strong-ly. Give the water direct from an open hose (but with slow water flow to prevent soil being washed off the roots) or from the spout of a watering can and be sure to give enough to soak well into the soil. If the ground has been properly prepared no feeding will be required for the first two or three months and after that it will depend on the time of year and the degree of growth being made (see page 19).

Growing in containers Climbing plants of all kinds can also be grown permanently in large containers. Tubs or planters holding 100 litres (22 gal) of soil are about the minimum for permanent climbers of any kind. It is better to use a soil-based, rather than a peat-based compost because of its longer life and greater capacity to hold a good reserve of plant food. If garden soil is used, at least one third its own bulk of peat should be mixed with it to ensure good aeration combined with reasonable moisture holding; also add a slow release compound fertilizer such as John Innes base at the rate advised by the manufacturer.

OPPOSITE, ABOVE Always plant climbers at least 30–45cm (1–1½ft) from a wall to avoid problems of dryness.

RIGHT Some climbers can also be trailers, and make excellent ground cover. Here, *Hedera colchica variegata* outlines a pathway while, in the container, another hedera begins to climb the new brick wall. Quite a number of climbers can be container grown.

HOW TO USE CLIMBERS

Climbers can be used to clothe walls or fences, or be allowed to cover arches and pergolas, or be trained up posts, pillars and tripods and over arbours and screens of many kinds or they may simply be permitted to find their own natural way among the branches of trees and shrubs. Sometimes one sturdy type of climber can be used to support a more fragile-stemmed climber, such as a clematis or a sweet pea, and these combinations can produce delightful effects. The use that is to be made of the plants will have a bearing both on their selection and on the way in which they are grown.

The prolifically flowering *Hydrangea petiolaris* (climbing hydrangea) provides attractive screening for a less than perfect wall or, as here, a tree stump. However, this vigorous self-clinger will require judicious cutting back from time to time where space is restricted.

Trees or shrubs used as supports for climbers. In such instances, it should not be overlooked that the hosts may be retarded by their companions. Ivy will ascend to the top of high trees and, though it does little harm in the early years, once it erupts from the top and commences to form a canopy it can soon kill the tree. The Russian Vine, *Polygonum baldschuanicum*, can also grow right over the top of trees and some very vigorous wild roses will do the same. They can look spectacular when their flowers cascade from a great height but it would be unwise to subject one's best trees to this kind of competition. Sometimes old orchard trees, no longer of much use for cropping, are worth retaining as living supports for the more moderately vigorous climbing or rambler roses and clematis. Many of the summer flowering varieties of clematis can be cut hard back each year, in late winter or early spring, and this restricts their growth sufficiently to make them very acceptable companions even for some medium size shrubs or they can be allowed to thread their way over a close carpet of heather. However, all such schemes require close attention to ensure that they do not get out of hand and a readiness to prune if there is any risk to the host plant.

Walls and fences can provide all the support necessary for self-clinging climbers such as ivies, ampelopsis and the climbing hydrangeas, *Hydrangea petiolaris, Schizophragma integrifolium, S. hydrangioides* and *Pileostegia viburnoides,* but with all these there is a danger that growth will extend too far and penetrate beneath tiles or block up gutters and waterpipes. The popular belief that such plants harm bricks, stones or concrete is false but they may hasten the decay of woodwork and, unless kept in check, can make painting and other maintenance work more difficult. Against this must be weighed the advantage that the plants will require no extra support, no nails, vine eyes or trellis, and that they will need virtually no maintenance except for occasional pruning simply to keep them within reasonable bounds.

ABOVE Semi- or full shade is best for *Lonicera tellmanniana,* a hybrid with orange-yellow, terminal clusters of flowers in mid-summer. A strong-growing, deciduous climber here lending its brightness to a pillar well suited to the plant's twining habit.

LEFT The evergreen Pyracanthas can be pruned to suit the requirements of their 'host'. This particularly well-trained *Pyracantha* 'Orange Glow' hugs the house wall without the sacrifice of berries that such pruning can demand.

Ugly walls can be made beautiful with climbers and those that are in poor condition may actually be preserved by the protection the foliage gives from frost, damp and atmospheric pollution.

Twiners and tendril climbers on walls will need some additional support. It can be wires strained between vine eyes driven into the masonry, trellis fixed in any convenient way but not pressed so tightly against the wall that stems or tendrils cannot get around it, or netting either of coated or galvanized wire or of nylon. Each has its merits and drawbacks but probably horizontal wires strained 2.5cm (1in) out from the wall and at about 30 cm (1ft) vertical spacing is as neat and convenient as anything.

To avoid making too many holes in a wall, it may be desirable to attach a wooden framework firmly to it and then fix the wires to the wood. What must always be borne in mind is that the weight of a vigorous climber is considerable and so the support, whatever its nature, must be firmly secured or in time it will inevitably collapse.

Other supports For the above reason flimsily built arches are also a menace. They need to be strong and firmly anchored in the soil. Pergolas must be sturdily constructed with substantial uprights and roof members. If wires are strained along each side of a pergola, climbers can be trained along them and the whole thing converted into a plant tunnel. Alternatively, plants can be confined to the pillars and the roof members, the interspaces between the uprights being left open to the air, rather in the manner of a cloister.

A mellow brick wall is an asset to be highlighted rather than concealed. And what could be more complementary than *Chaenomeles speciosa*, with clusters of fiery red flowers in early spring and greenish-yellow edible fruits in autumn. When it is wall-trained, this climber should be pruned after its flowering.

Climbers grown on single vertical poles can be convenient since they occupy little lateral space but the poles need to be deeply sunk in the soil if they are to remain upright for long when burdened with growth. It is easier to obtain stability with tripods lashed or nailed together at the top but, inevitably, these occupy a good deal more ground.

A considerable variety of arbours can be purchased and all can be used as supports for climbers if so desired. Metal arbours are more likely to survive for a long time than wooden ones and tendril climbers will find the relatively slim metal bars congenial for support. All wood used for supporting plants should be rot proof either by its own nature, for example, western red cedar or an African hardwood, or through impregnation with a rot repellant. Creosote is best avoided as in hot weather it can give off fumes that scorch plants. However, this danger is much greater under glass than outdoors.

Whole patios or courtyards, or sections of them, can be covered with climbers to make pleasant outdoor rooms. The roof can be formed of rafters in a similar manner to a pergola or with strained wire but even stout wire is apt to sag in time if the spans are greater than 1.2m (4ft). Much depends on the type of climber chosen and the degree of pruning it receives. Vines heavily pruned both in winter and summer make a fairly light yet attractive canopy for a sitting-out area.

ABOVE A really well-constructed pergola provides an ideal framework for the more rampant climbers. *Rosa* 'Seagull' with its lovely, massed flowers is one such grateful tenant.

LEFT Another popular climbing rose, 'American Pillar' clambers up its sturdy support, forming an archway of deep pink flowerheads.

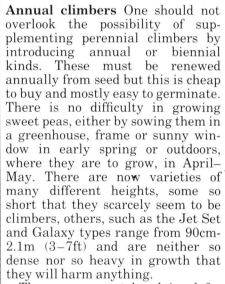

Annual climbers One should not overlook the possibility of supplementing perennial climbers by introducing annual or biennial kinds. These must be renewed annually from seed but this is cheap to buy and mostly easy to germinate. There is no difficulty in growing sweet peas, either by sowing them in a greenhouse, frame or sunny window in early spring or outdoors, where they are to grow, in April–May. There are now varieties of many different heights, some so short that they scarcely seem to be climbers, others, such as the Jet Set and Galaxy types range from 90cm-2.1m (3–7ft) and are neither so dense nor so heavy in growth that they will harm anything.

The same cannot be claimed for climbing nasturtiums which make a lot of growth and have quite big leaves that exclude a lot of light. But they grow at express speed, their scarlet, orange and yellow colours are very bright and seed can be sown outdoors from mid-April to mid-May where the plants are to bloom. Nasturtiums are ideal to make a dense screen or cover for unsightly objects.

Another very fast growing climber to raise from seed is *Cobaea scandens*. It is really a perennial but seldom survives the winter outdoors in Britain and grows so rapidly from seed that it is usually treated as a half-hardy annual. This means sowing in a warm greenhouse in February-March, potting the seedlings individually and acclimatizing them so that they can be planted outdoors safely in late May or early June. The flowers are rather like those of Canterbury Bells – in fact the popular name is Cathedral Bells – and they are either purple or greenish-white. There are seldom enough of them to be spectacular but they look very pretty peeping out among other things. *Eccremocarpus scaber*, popularly known as the Glory Flower, though strictly a soft-stemmed perennial, is also often grown as a half-hardy annual in the same way as a cobaea. It has much divided ferny leaves and slender stems provided with tendrils and abundant little tubular flowers in orange, yellow or red, all summer.

The Morning Glories, of which the best are *Ipomaea* 'Heavenly Blue', wholly blue, and *I.* 'Flying Saucers', blue and white, are very spectacular when doing well but they need warmth and sunshine to bring out their best. They are genuine half-hardy annuals, needing the same

treatment as cobaea but with more warmth, around 24°C, 75°F for germination. Young plants of both cobaea and ipomaea can be purchased in most garden centres in May-June. Unfortunately, eccremocarpus is seldom on offer.

Yet another useful, fast-growing climber is the annual hop, *Humulus japonicus*, which can reach 4.5m (15ft) in a few months. It has little beauty of flower but the leaves are handsome and there is a white variegated variety. It is hardy and so can be sown outdoors, in a sunny position. In fact, once established it is likely to produce many self-sown seedlings which may become a nuisance. Do not confuse this plant with the perennial hop which will live for years and has a beautiful golden leaved variety.

OPPOSITE, FAR LEFT *Cotoneaster horizontalis* vies for attention with the equally bright *Jasminum nudiflorum*; a stunning combination. But the Jasmine needs firm control.

OPPOSITE, NEAR LEFT The rather tender *Fremontia californica,* teamed here with *Euryops pectinata* and *Rosa anemoides.*

ABOVE *Ipomaea purpurea* can be spectacular when given the right conditions.

RIGHT Fast-growing *Humulus japonica* 'Aureus' taking a pergola in its stride.

Regular care Climbing and rambler roses (the main difference between them is that the ramblers are laxer in growth and make more of their new stems from the base) are trained against walls, on fences or on poles, pillars, tripods, arches and pergolas. In all these places their stems must be tied in regularly or they will flop all over the place. The only way in which they can become self-supporting, or largely so, is when planted beside trees or shrubs into which they can scramble. Some ramblers, of which 'Max Graff' is a well known example, are sometimes grown as ground cover with no support of any kind or are allowed to tumble down steep banks.

What has been said of the climbing roses is also true of all the other thrusters or scramblers which, in the wild, either sprawl or find support among other stiffer stemmed plants. If this is not a convenient way to grow them in the garden their stems must be tied regularly to any of the supports suggested for roses. Tying in is a time consuming task and, with roses and the ornamental brambles, often a prickly one, though there are thornless or nearly thornless varieties. It is particularly necessary to keep all these plants under control if they are grown on house walls or used to cover arches and pergolas.

Flowers and foliage When choosing climbing plants, most people will think of their flowers first. Yet flowers rarely last for long. The wonderful display of wisteria, for example, is over in a couple of weeks and the highly popular *Clematis montana* only retains its flowers for about a week longer. Most of the garden varieties of clematis have a much longer season though it can be patchy just as the so-called repeat flowering roses concentrate most of their display in a few summer weeks with much smaller but very welcome quantities of bloom later.

By contrast, foliage is there for much longer, all the year if it is evergreen and for at least six months if it is deciduous. The leaves of vines and of the related ampelopsis are beautiful in shape and some kinds colour richly before they fall in the autumn. Actinidias are grown solely for their leaves and so, of course, are ivies except when they start to flower and fruit and then they turn bushy and cease to climb. It is wise to consider this carefully when choosing climbers for the garden and include a fair proportion that have good foliage.

Fruits Also one should think of fruits and ripening seeds for autumn effect. Most spectacular are the scarlet- and orange-berried Firethorns (pyracantha) which are shrubs, not climbers, but readily trained against walls. *Cotoneaster horizontalis* is also a shrub which spreads horizontally in the open but will flatten itself like a fan against a wall when it serves the same purpose as a climber and needs no support. It has neat little leaves which turn coppery red before they fall in the autumn, at which season it is also covered with bright red berries.

Celastrus orbiculatus is grown for its scarlet seeds, displayed against yellow seed capsules, and some clematis cover their seeds with beautiful silken filaments which aid their widespread distribution by wind.

FAR LEFT *Rosa* 'Golden Showers', a beauty well worth regular care.

LEFT *Clematis montana* 'Tetra Rose' tends to grow tall before branching out.

ABOVE Undemanding *Cotoneaster horizontalis* makes a colourful hedge or self-supporting wall plant.

RIGHT Delicate but lovely and prolific, Lathyrus, here cordon grown.

AFTERCARE AND PRUNING

The two things most likely to prevent climbers from getting a good start are dryness and wind. Walls, fences and even pergolas are likely to deflect some rain, so making the soil close to them drier than it would otherwise be. Walls and fences can also cause strong draughts and unexpected turbulence. So in the early stages it may be necessary to water freely and frequently and it may also be desirable to shelter the young growth a little with fine mesh nylon netting or anything similar that will break the force of the wind without stifling the plants.

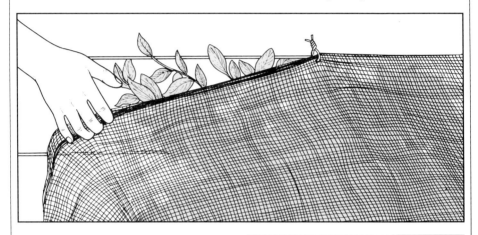

Winter protection Later on, as roots spread out widely, climbers will be able to look after themselves most of the time but there may be some rather tender kinds, such as the Passion Flower *(Passiflora caerulea)*, the Potato Vines *(Solanum crispum* and *S. jasminoides)* and the Trumpet Vines *(Tecoma radicans* and *T. Mdme. Galen)* which, in all but the mildest parts of Britain, will benefit from some protection every winter. One of the advantages of growing plants against walls is the ease with which they can be protected by draping fine-mesh netting over them. Also, remain watchful for severe dryness near walls and beneath trees. It is sometimes necessary to leave a hose or a sprinkler running for a while to restore good growing conditions.

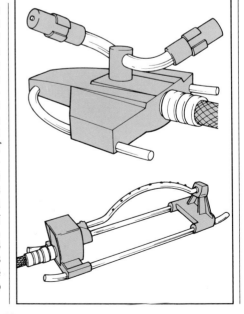

Feeding It is easy to forget this and equally easy to forget that climbers, just like other plants, need food. There are some vigorous kinds, such as wisterias and Russian Vine *(Polygonum baldschuanicum)*, that will scarcely ever need any extra encouragement but at the other extreme the very large-flowered varieties of clematis can do with a lot of help. For success they rely on strong new growth each spring and summer and without feeding they are unlikely to make it.

The same is true of climbing and rambler roses though the real monsters, like Kiftsgate, *Rosa multiflora, R. filipes* and *R. longicuspis*, belong to the self-help league.

Both organics and inorganics have a part to play. The really bulky organics, such as farmyard manure, stable manure, garden compost and old mushroom compost, used as thick top dressings, are most useful if spread while the soil is still moist from winter rain. Inorganic fertilizers as liquid or granules are applied occasionally as a light dressing between April and August.

There is seldom any need to use anything out of the ordinary. A well balanced nitrogen, phosphorus and potash fertilizer such as ICI Liquid Growmore or ordinary granular Growmore will meet most requirements. The liquid is diluted as advised and applied from a can; the granules are lightly peppered over the surface for about 90cm (3ft) around the base of each plant, a first application in April with more to follow in early June and late July when demand will be at its height.

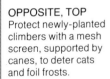

OPPOSITE, TOP Protect newly-planted climbers with a mesh screen, supported by canes, to deter cats and foil frosts.

LEFT A sprinkler soon repays the investment.

RIGHT Slow to establish itself but then a true climber, *Rosa* 'Kiftsgate' – here trained on a frame – would just as happily climb a tree unaided. But make sure that the tree is up to the challenge; those enormous trusses of flowers are very heavy!

Tying is only essential for those plants that do not twist or cling of their own accord. Roses are by far the most numerous and important and, if not carefully and regularly tied in they can become a nuisance. Since there is a constant renewal of growth with these, as with the ornamental brambles, string is as good a material as any for tying. It does not last very long but it does not need to do so and has the great advantage of being very easy to cut and remove.

A difficulty with roses is that, though it is easiest to tie with bare fingers, these are terribly exposed to sharp thorns. It is much easier with two people, one wearing thorn-proof gloves and holding the stems in position, while the other ties them in barehanded. The best compromise, if no helper is available, is to wear tough but flexible gloves which may not give full protection but make it possible to tie a knot. Some may prefer to use flexible wire which can be twisted with one hand. There are also numerous proprietary ties, some very effective but most rather expensive if you need several.

Pruning The most important maintenance task with climbers is pruning. It is almost impossible to grow roses satisfactorily without it and bad pruning can ruin the result. The quality of bloom of garden varieties of clematis can be improved by pruning and the performance of wistarias is also considerably influenced. Vines must be pruned to prevent them becoming a dense tangle of growth and ivies must be prevented from suffocating other plants. Most of this work is much easier than some of the experts make it appear.

ROSES Though stems will survive for many years, getting thicker and harder in the process, it is the young growth, much of it no more than one year old, that produces most of the good flowers. So each winter one tries to cut out as many of the older stems as possible without losing too much young growth.

With vigorous ramblers such as 'American Pillar' and 'Dorothy Perkins' this is easy since they make a lot of long, young stems from near the base. During the summer these

LEFT A wooden trellis, securely fixed to the wall by means of battens, allows air to circulate behind the foliage. Essential for climbers without their own support system, such as the semi-hardy *Abutilon vitifolium* 'Veronica Tennant'.

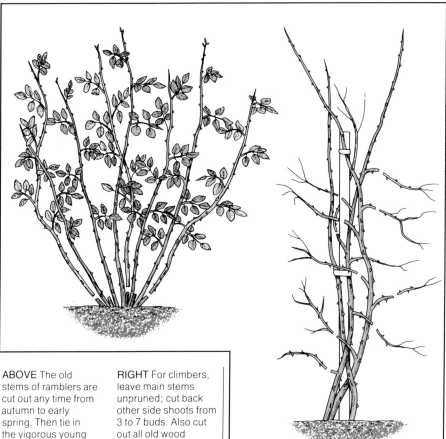

ABOVE The old stems of ramblers are cut out any time from autumn to early spring. Then tie in the vigorous young ones to replace them.

RIGHT For climbers, leave main stems unpruned; cut back other side shoots from 3 to 7 buds. Also cut out all old wood where possible.

can be tied to one side away from the flowering stems and then, when all the flowers have faded or at any time after that until the following March, the old stems can be cut out and the vigorous young ones tied in to take their place.

Many climbing roses, especially those that flower most of the summer, do not make such a clear distinction between old and new growth. Some of the good new stems may come from the base but many branch out from old stems, higher up, and so one must compromise. The aim is still to cut out as much as possible of the old wood but some of

this can only be cut back as far as the good new growth coming from it. One must study the space available and go on cutting out and tying in until it is comfortably filled with healthy young growth. What remains can then be removed.

The ornamental brambles more or less settle the matter for themselves since they allow their old stems to die when they have finished their year; it is then quite clear that they need to be cut out. Some of the weaker young stems can be removed with them if there are too many developing stems left for the amount of space that is available.

CLEMATIS thrive on young growth on which all the flowers are carried. Those that do not start to flower until mid-June or later can, if desired, be cut hard back each February-March, even to within 30cm (1ft) of ground level. This will reduce the size of the plant but may also increase the size of the flowers. Even in February, growth is usually starting so it is easy to see where one can make a pruning cut and be sure of getting a new shoot. This early pruning is not feasible with spring and early summer flowering kinds which have by then made the growth from which they will flower but they can be considerably thinned or cut back immediately after flowering if they threaten to occupy too much space.

HONEYSUCKLES All the popular honeysuckles produce their flowers in a slightly different way, carried on short new growth which comes direct from much longer stems made the previous year. Often they can be left to fend for themselves with little or no pruning but if they start to lose vigour this can be restored by cutting out some of the older growth immediately the flowers fade and supplementing this by feeding and watering. Where space is restricted, honeysuckles can be pruned annually after flowering but with care to preserve plenty of the new growth which will be in evidence by then.

ABOVE
Honeysuckles are fairly self-sufficient, space-invaders; if pruning becomes necessary, take care to preserve the new growth.

RIGHT Two *Clematis* × *Jackmanii* frame a window with their huge, deep violet flower heads. *C. viticella* (far right) should be hard pruned in February or March.

WISTERIAS AND VINES flower on young side growths and plants can be allowed to make a permanent framework of old stems that will get increasingly thick and woody with age. From this side growths are allowed to form but in summer each is shortened to about 15cm (6in). For extra neatness, these pruned shoots can be further shortened to about 2.5cm (1in) in winter. By these means these normally rather rampant climbers can be restricted to quite small areas.

SHRUBS that are trained against walls or fences must be pruned to alter their shape from all-round branching to growth virtually in one plane only. Most of this can be done in summer, after the plants have flowered. Then any good stems for which there is space, and which are sufficiently well placed or flexible to be tied in, are retained.

Other stems for which there is no room or which grow too stiffly away from wall or fence are either cut right out or are shortened to a few centimetres/inches. This is particularly useful with ceanothus, chaenomeles and pyracantha, all of which make flower buds freely on such shortened stems. By contrast, *Forsythia suspensa* and chimonanthus flower better on long stems and so it will be helpful to get as much as possible of this tied in at full length. When pruning fruit-bearing shrubs, retain as much as possible of the fruit and by June-July it will be possible to see where this is.

General care Many climbers can be left unpruned for years but always remove dead or damaged growth as soon as it is noted. If a plant grows too far it can be thinned or cut back as necessary, the best time for this being February–March unless the

TOP Vines need careful, systematic pruning if they are to give of their best.

ABOVE *Forsythia suspensa* and *Clematis alpina*. The former needs tieing in.

plant flowers in spring or early summer when it is better to leave pruning until after flowering. Ivies can be cut back at any time and, when grown on walls, can be freshened up in May–June by clipping them with shears or hedge trimmers. Then the plant can be well brushed to rid it of accumulated debris, which can be considerable.

PROPAGATION

Because of their long, flexible stems it is often quite easy to increase climbing plants by layering. Some will even do it for themselves, making roots from stems which remain in contact with the soil for a considerable time. Quite apart from this obliging – and occasionally irritating – self-sufficiency, climbers can quickly and economically be propagated from cuttings. If you have patience, and in some cases perseverance, they can also be successfully raised from seed.

The best time for layering a clematis is May to June. Gently bend the selected stem and peg down as described in the text (below left). Leave until the following March before detaching from the parent and transplanting.

Layering While climbers will often root from stems of their own accord, the process can be made more reliable by selecting stems one or two years old, making a small wound in each at a joint that can be brought down to the soil and then burying this 2.5cm (1in) or so deep and holding it firmly in place with a stone or peg. A joint is the point at which a leaf is, or was, attached to a stem and it is from this that roots are most readily formed. A wound restricts the flow of sap and promotes root formation. The most efficient methods of wounding for this purpose are either to make a slit through the joint or to draw a knife round the stem just below the joint, cutting sufficiently deep to penetrate the skin without severing the stem. Root formation can be hastened by dusting the wound with hormone rooting powder or dabbing it with a rooting solution or gel.

Layers can be made at any time of year but late spring/early summer is usually a favourable time. When the layer has made some good roots, which is unlikely to be in less than a year, it can be severed from its parent, lifted carefully with as much soil as possible still around them and replanted elsewhere.

Cuttings can be quicker than layers and require much less material. They should be prepared from 12–15cm (4–6in) long pieces of firm current year's growth (it is usually necessary to wait until July for this) and should be severed immediately below a joint. The lower leaves are then removed, the base of the cutting is dipped in rooting powder, liquid or gel and inserted in a half and half mixture of peat and either perlite or gritty sand in a small flower pot. This should then be placed in a propagator or in a polythene bag sealed to retain moist air inside. The cuttings, whether in a propagator or bags, should have plenty of light but it is best not to expose them to strong direct sunlight which may scorch them. As soon as roots begin to form, growth will resume; a few weeks later the cuttings can be potted individually in a peat or soil-based potting compost and grown on until large enough to be planted out where they are to grow. There are advantages in keeping them in a frame until they are sturdy enough to thrive outside.

Seed Some climbers can also be raised from seed which is usually best sown as soon as ripe but if this is impossible, sow the following spring. It is best to sow in pans or seed trays and any standard peat or soil-based seed compost can be used. The seeds can be germinated out of doors or in a greenhouse or frame. Germination of some species can be slow and erratic so do not throw away seed containers for at least eighteen months, and keep looking.

ABOVE Hederas will happily propagate themselves – rooting wherever a trailing stem touches soil. But if you want to speed up the process, any number of stem cuttings can be taken and then planted six to a pot.

LEFT Sowing seeds of climbers in peat pots means that you can plant them out without root disturbance, later.

PESTS AND DISEASES

Climbers suffer from many of the pests and diseases that afflict other plants but, with the exception of some varieties of rose, are not often severely affected. Mildews, rusts and leaf spots of various kinds may infect them and greenfly, blackfly and other aphids may suck the sap from their young shoots and leaves.

No one chemical will deal with all of these but some manufacturers prepare mixtures of pesticides with a wide spectrum of efficacy. An excellent example is 'Roseclear', manufactured by ICI which, as its name implies, has been prepared primarily for roses but can be used safely and effectively on all ornamental climbing plants. It provides a simple method of dealing with all greenfly or blackfly or fungal diseases likely to be encountered. Alternatively, to control other pests, 'Sybol' can be used alone or in a mixture with 'Nimrod'–T or Benlate + 'Activex' for combined pest and disease control. If desired, the two can be mixed in the same sprayer.

If such all-embracing remedies are applied at least three times a year, first in May, again in June and a third time in late July or early August, there should not be much to worry about. But here are a few more specific recommendations regarding the more common pests and diseases for those who prefer not to use blanket treatments.

Aphids The name covers greenfly and blackfly which are slow moving and likely to be found mainly on the new growth. Aphids can multiply at a prodigious rate when conditions are favourable, particularly from May-September. Pirimicarb, marketed as 'Rapid', can kill them within 30 minutes and does not affect other insects, including the industrious bees and ladybirds.

Aphids on rose bud.

Red Spider Mites These are so small that a lens may be required to identify them. They live mainly on the undersides of leaves, particularly along the veins, and they thrive in hot, dry weather when there may be so many of them sucking sap that leaves become mottled with grey or yellow. Many of the insecticides in common use do not kill these tiny mites but pirimiphos-methyl, available as 'Sybol', will. Thorough spraying or hosing with water will also reduce numbers of mites greatly as they hate dampness.

'Sybol' can also be used to control other garden pests if they look like becoming a problem.

26

Mildew Leaves and sometimes stems become covered with white or grey powdery mould. This is common on roses, especially when the air is damp and the soil dry, and may also be troublesome on vines. Spraying with 'Nimrod'-T or Benlate + 'Activex' will control it.

Rust Another fairly common rose disease. The undersides of leaves are covered with little orange spots and the leaves turn yellow and drop. Spraying with 'Nimrod'-T as soon as rust is noticed gives control.

Advanced stage of mildew.

Black Spot Specific to roses and common on some varieties. Black spots appear on the leaves and rapidly extend to cover and destroy them. Spraying with 'Nimrod'-T or Benlate + 'Activex' will give control but it is wise to alternate these fungicides to prevent the emergence of resistant strains of the fungus.

Weevils Most likely to be troublesome on vines. Black beetle-like insects eat holes in the leaves and larvae feed on the roots. Either spray the foliage or drench the soil with 'Sybol'.

Clematis Wilt Leaves and young stems suddenly collapse. Once every fortnight in April and May spray with Benlate + 'Activex' or a copper fungicide such as Bordeaux Mixture.

Leaf-rolling Sawfly Sometimes widespread on roses. Leaves roll up lengthwise due to attack by small grubs. As a preventive, spray the foliage with 'Sybol'.

Black Spot, specific to roses.

Leaf-rolling Sawfly.

27

CHOICE CLIMBERS

Whether you want to provide privacy in a town garden, lend fragrance to a patio, draw attention to a mellow brick wall, graceful arbour or stylish pergola – or simply perhaps to blot out a sore on the landscape that cannot be literally removed – there's more than one willing and able climber to meet your needs. Here is a selection of the choicest, each with its special attributes, all sure to give lasting pleasure and widely available at garden centres.

Abutilon megapotamicum

Deciduous shrub. A slender stemmed plant that will sprawl unless tied to a support. It is excellent for a sunny wall against which it can grow 1.8m (6ft) high and produce an abundance of little yellow and red lantern shaped flowers all summer. It will survive a little frost but may be cut to ground level or even killed in severe winters.

Abutilon vitifolium

Deciduous shrub. A tall, rather sparsely branched shrub that can be trained against a sunny wall. The leaves are vine-shaped and covered with down, the mallow-type flowers are soft violet or white and come in June–July. It is fairly hardy but not usually long lived, though readily renewable either from seed or from summer cuttings.

Actinidia chinensis

Deciduous twiner. Popularly known as Chinese Gooseberry because of its edible fruits but these are only produced by female plants in the presence of a male. It is most valuable for its large rounded leaves and stems covered in red hairs when young. It can easily reach 9m (30ft) and is useful for quick coverage of unsightly objects and to give a sub-tropical effect. Will grow in full sun or light shade.

Actinidia kolomikta

Deciduous twiner. A much more slender stemmed plant than the last, grown for its leaves which are heavily splashed with pink and cream when young. It is at its best in May–June. It will reach 3m (10ft), likes sun and warmth and is fairly hardy but young leaves and shoots may be damaged by frost in spring.

Azara microphylla

Evergreen shrub. A slenderly branched shrub with small, dark green leaves and little tufts of yellow, very sweetly scented flowers in winter and early spring. There is a variety with cream variegated leaves. It is a little tender and so best trained against a south- or west-facing wall.

Distinctive mallow-type flowers of Abutilon megapotamicum.

Actinidia kolomikta

Camellia reticulata

Evergreen shrub. The long stems lend themselves to training against a wall and this is often the best place for this handsome camellia which is just a little tender. 'Captain Rawes', with very large, semi-double carmine flowers in March-April, is a fine form.

Ceanothus impressus

Evergreen shrub. In the open this makes a densely branched bush but with careful pruning and tying it can be trained against a wall. It is one of the hardiest and most beautiful of the Californian Lilacs which produces abundant thimble-shaped clusters of small, scented, deep blue flowers in April–May. 'Puget Blue' is a good form and very popular. Plant in a sunny position.

Ceanothus thyrsiflorus

Evergreen shrub. A much taller, less widely branched shrub than the last, and therefore easier to train against a wall, but the blue flowers are not quite such a fine colour. It can reach a height of 6m (20ft). A variety named 'Cascade' has larger flower clusters and arching stems which must be allowed some freedom.

Ceanothus veitchianus

Evergreen shrub. Much like the last but the leaves are a brighter green and the flowers a deeper blue. It is not likely to grow quite so tall.

Celastrus orbiculatus

Deciduous twiner. A very vigorous plant excellent for quick coverage of unsightly buildings. It is grown for its seed pods which are unremarkable until they split open to reveal scarlet seeds on a yellow interior. It is essential to obtain the hermaphrodite form which bears both male and female flowers or there will be no seeds. This form must be increased by layers or cuttings since seedlings may be of one sex only.

Ceanothus thyrsiflorus

Chaenomeles speciosa **'Moerloosii'**

Chaenomeles speciosa

Deciduous shrub. This is the shrub many people know as 'Japonica'. It is a Japanese quince which produces its bright red flowers from December until April and follows them with large, scented fruits. There are numerous colour variations such as 'Nivalis', white; 'Moerloosii', also called 'Apple Blossom', pink and white and 'Rubra Grandiflora', crimson. All will grow and flower in full sun or semi-shade. Considerable pruning is required to deal with their abundant growth.

Chimonanthus praecox

Deciduous shrub. This is the Winter Sweet, so called because of the very sweet perfume of its not very conspicuous greenish-yellow and purple flowers from January to March. It benefits from the protection of a sunny wall against which it is easy to train its long stems.

Chimonanthus fragrans

Clematis 'Hagley Hybrid'

Clematis alpina
Deciduous, tendril climber. This is very different from the popular image of a clematis. The flowers are small, skirt-shaped and nodding, blue or light pink with a tuft of white in the centre; they come in April–May. 'Francis Revis' is a good blue and white variety. All forms grow to about 2.4m (8ft) high.

Clematis armandii
Evergreen tendril climber. This grows strongly, will reach 6m (20ft) and has clusters of small white flowers in April. The leaves are long, shining green and handsome. A specially good form is 'Snowdrift'. The plant is just a little tender and a south- or south-west-facing wall suits it well.

Clematis 'Comtesse de Bouchaud'
Deciduous, tendril climber. Large, soft pink flowers from June to August. Moderately vigorous growth.

Clematis 'Ernest Markham'
Deciduous, tendril climber. Large, petunia-purple flowers from June to September. Moderately vigorous.

Clematis 'Hagley Hybrid'
Deciduous, tendril climber. Large, light pink flowers from June to September. Moderately vigorous.

Clematis 'Lasurstern'

Clematis 'Huldine'
Deciduous, tendril climber. Large white flowers, mauve on the underside, from July to October. Moderately vigorous.

Clematis flammula
Deciduous, tendril climber. Abundant small, white, scented flowers in huge clusters from August to October. Vigorous. Will reach 3.5m (12ft) or more.

Clematis jackmanii
Deciduous, tendril climber. Abundant, medium size, violet-purple flowers from July to October. A variety named 'Superba' has larger iris-purple flowers.

Clematis 'Lasurstern'
Deciduous, tendril climber. Very large lavender-blue flowers in May and June and some smaller flowers later. Moderately vigorous.

33

Clematis macropetala
Deciduous, tendril climber. A little like *C. alpina* but the flowers are filled with small, petal-like segments making them resemble a ballerina's tutu. Typically the flowers are light violet-blue but 'Markham's Pink' has light rose flowers. All will reach 2.4m (8ft).

Clematis 'Marie Boisselot'
Deciduous, tendril climber. Large, broad-petalled white flowers appear from May to October. A moderately vigorous variety.

Clematis montana
Deciduous, tendril climber. Very vigorous with abundant small white or soft pink flowers which in some forms are scented. Can reach 9m (30ft). Colour and quality of bloom vary a lot so it is best to buy selected varieties such as 'Grandiflora', white and 'Rubens', pink.

Clematis 'Mrs Cholmondeley'
Deciduous, tendril climber. Very large, lavender-blue flowers from May to August. Moderately vigorous.

Clematis 'Ville de Lyon'

Clematis 'Perle D'Azur'

Clematis 'Nelly Moser'
Deciduous, tendril climber. Very large mauve flowers with carmine bars in May–June, with sometimes a few to follow later. Moderate vigour.

Clematis orientalis
Deciduous, tendril climber. Small, yellow, thick-petalled flowers in August followed by silvery seed heads. A very vigorous plant which will reach 6m (20ft).

Clematis 'Perle d'Azur'
Deciduous, tendril climber. Medium size, light blue flowers very freely produced from late June until late August. Fairly vigorous.

Clematis 'Royal Velours'
Deciduous, tendril climber. Small, deep reddish-purple flowers very freely produced in August and September. A vigorous plant.

Clematis tangutica
Deciduous, tendril climber. Small, yellow flowers in August–September, followed by silvery seed heads. Can reach 4m (13ft).

Clematis orientalis with seed heads

Clematis 'The President'
Deciduous, tendril climber. Very large purplish-blue flowers from June through to September. Moderate vigour.

Clematis 'Ville de Lyon'
Deciduous, tendril climber. Large carmine flowers from July to August. Moderate vigour.

Cotoneaster horizontalis
Deciduous shrub. Out in the open this shrub will spread out horizontally but if planted by a wall or fence it will fan out against it and give complete cover to a height of about 2.4m (8ft) without any support. The small leaves colour brilliantly before they fall in the autumn and the deep red berries are retained for a long time. The white flowers in June are much visited by honey bees.

Cytisus battandieri
Deciduous shrub. The long flexible stems of this 4m (13ft) Moroccan broom can be trained easily against a wall and it enjoys a warm sunny place. The leaves are covered in silky down and the erect clusters of yellow flowers that appear in May and in June are pineapple scented.

Euonymus fortunei radicans
Self-clinging evergreen. This very distinctive plant has rather small but very numerous leaves and stems which lie flat on the ground, rooting into it, but against a wall or fence will ascend, using the stem roots to cling like ivy. It can reach a height of 6m (20ft) and will thrive in sun or shade. A variety named 'Variegatus' has grey-green leaves edged with white – and often tinged pink.

Cytisus battandieri

Fremontodendron 'California Glory'

Euonymus fortunei 'Silver Queen'

Evergreen shrub. Unlike the last, this makes no stem roots and so cannot climb of its own accord but it can be trained to a height of about 2.4m (8ft). The leaves are quite large, shining green and heavily variegated with white. An invaluable shrub for enlivening the garden in the dark, winter months.

Wall-trained *Ficus carica*.

Fatshedera lizei

Evergreen sprawler. This hybrid between fatsia and ivy has large, deeply-lobed, evergreen leaves and long floppy stems which can be tied to any support to reach a height of about 2m (6ft). It will grow in sun or shade and is an excellent plant with which to give a sub-tropical effect to a patio or courtyard.

Ficus carica

Evergreen shrub. This is the common fig, a vigorous shrub frequently trained against walls where it is most likely to ripen its fruits. It is worth growing solely for its large, glossy, evergreen, deeply-lobed leaves, which are very handsome. It will grow in sun or shade but its fruits will only ripen in a warm, sunny place. It can reach 3m (10ft).

Forsythia suspensa

Deciduous shrub. This has the longest, most flexible stems of any forsythia and so is the best for training against walls. The flowers, which come in March–April, are light yellow and there is a variety, named 'Atrocaulis', with pale yellow flowers and purple stems which become almost black as they age.

Fremontodendron 'California Glory'

Evergreen shrub. The long stems of this free-flowering shrub can be trained to a height of about 6m (20ft). The leaves are slightly bronzy-green; the big, saucer-shaped flowers, from May to July, are bright yellow. This plant is not fully hardy but if trained against a south- or west-facing wall it will usually survive all but the most severe winters in milder parts of Britain. However, it is not naturally long lived and you may find that it has to be renewed from time to time.

Garrya elliptica

Evergreen shrub. This distinctive shrub has long grey-green catkins that develop in winter and remain for several months. There are male and female forms but the males give the best flower display. Garrya benefits from the protection of a south- or west-facing wall and is sufficiently sturdy to hold itself up but wires or trellis will be required on which to spread out the young stems.

Hedera canariensis 'Variegata'

Catkins of Garrya elliptica.

Hedera canariensis 'Variegata'

Self-clinging evergreen. A beautiful form of the Canary Island ivy, the leaves variegated with grey-green and cream. It is not as hardy as the British ivy but is excellent for sheltered patios and courtyards.

Hedera colchica 'Dentata Variegata'

Self-clinging evergreen. A large-leaved, fully hardy ivy with bold grey-green and creamy yellow variegation. It will thrive in either sun or shade.

Hedera helix 'Buttercup'

Self-clinging evergreen. A good all-yellow variety of the common ivy. It will grow in shade but leaf colour is best in good light and particularly on young leaves.

Hedera helix 'Goldheart'

Self-clinging evergreen. Another fine variety of the common ivy with a yellow blotch in the centre of each neat, dark green leaf. It colours best in good light.

Hedera helix 'Sagittifolia'

Self-clinging evergreen. Yet another variety of common ivy, distinguished by its rather small and narrow, five-lobed leaves.

37

Humulus lupulus 'Aureus'

Humulus lupulus 'Aureus'

A herbaceous twiner and the yellow-leaved form of the common hop, a hardy plant that dies down each autumn but is capable of making 4m (13ft) of growth the following spring and summer. Sunshine is required to produce the best leaf colour. Excellent for arbours, screens and so on where winter cover is not required.

Hydrangea petiolaris

Deciduous, self-clinging climber. The climbing hydrangea is very vigorous though rather slow starting and is capable eventually of reaching the top of a quite tall tree. It is also excellent on walls, whether sunny or shady. It clings by aerial roots like ivy and in June produces abundant flat clusters of white 'lacecap' flowers.

Jasminum nudiflorum

Deciduous sprawler. This is the popular Winter Jasmine with yellow flowers from November until March. Left to its own devices it will sprawl but its stems can be readily tied to any support and against a wall it will reach 4m (13ft). Because the stems are green, the plant looks evergreen but in fact the little three-parted leaves fall in the autumn.

Jasminum officinale

Jasminum officinale

Deciduous twiner. This is the sweet scented jasmine which for centuries has been a popular plant for growing over arbours and summerhouses or training around a porch. The white flowers come successively from June to October. There is a variety named 'Argenteovariegata' with grey-green leaves edged with white.

Kerria japonica 'Pleniflora'

Deciduous shrub. This garden variety makes fewer but much longer stems than the single flowered kerria and also has fully double, orange-yellow flowers, for which reason it is often called Batchelor's Buttons. It is easily trained on a wall, fence or screen and makes an excellent display in May–June. It will thrive in sun or semi-shade.

Lathyrus latifolius
Herbaceous tendril climber. This strong growing plant, which can cover a considerable area in a single season, is known as the Everlasting Pea because it is a long lived perennial. Typically the flowers are rose-pink but there are lighter pink and white varieties. All can be increased by seed or by division in the spring.

Lonicera americana
Deciduous twiner. Despite its name, this fine honeysuckle has no connection with America. It is a natural hybrid between two European species and has fragrant yellow flowers flushed with reddish-purple in June–July. Vigorous.

Lonicera brownii
Semi-evergreen twiner. Another vigorous hybrid honeysuckle, often called the Scarlet Trumpet Honeysuckle because of the shape and colour of its flowers. They have no scent and come in May with more to follow in August.

Lonicera japonica
Evergreen twiner. Two forms of this are grown in gardens: 'Halliana', with green leaves and very fragrant

Lonicera × tellmanniana

white flowers which become light yellow with age and 'Aureoreticulata', with leaves heavily netted with yellow.

Lonicera periclymenum
Deciduous twiner. Fine native honeysuckle with spicily fragrant flowers. Two forms are grown, 'Early Dutch' or 'Belgica' and 'Late Dutch' or 'Serotina' but it is difficult to distinguish between them. Both have purplish-red and yellow flowers in June and 'Late Dutch' can be expected to produce more later in the summer.

Lonicera × tellmanniana
Deciduous twiner. A distinctive and vigorous hybrid honeysuckle with abundant, scentless, yellow flowers in June–July.

Lonicera tragophylla
Deciduous twiner. One of the parents of the last named with even larger, scentless, yellow flowers in June–July. It is even more resentful than most honeysuckles of hot, dry soil. Grows to 6m (20ft).

Lathyrus latifolius

Magnolia grandiflora

Evergreen tree. It may seem strange to include a tree among wall shrubs but in fact this handsome magnolia trains well and is frequently grown on sunny walls where there is 4 to 5m (13 to 16ft) of height available. It is valued primarily for its large, shining evergreen leaves but also for the great bowl-shaped white flowers in August–September which are more likely to be produced freely in a warm sunny place. 'Goliath' is a particularly good variety.

Magnolia grandiflora

Parthenocissus henryana

Deciduous, self-clinging climber. This is one of those ornamental vines that gardeners are apt to lump together as Virginia Creepers. Its leaves, composed of several radiating leaflets, are dark green, pink and white. The plant is provided with adhesive pads which enable it to cling to anything. It is just a little tender but is ideal for a west-facing wall in a not too cold area.

Self-clinging *Parthenocissus henryana*.

Parthenocissus quinquefolia

Deciduous, tendril climber. This is the true Virginia Creeper, a very vigorous plant with large, five-lobed leaves which colour vividly in autumn. It cannot cling to walls but, with the aid of tendrils, will mount high into trees or go far over screens and pergolas.

Parthenocissus tricuspidata

Deciduous, self-clinging climber. The true popular name for this is Boston Ivy but it is often called Virginia Creeper or Ampelopsis. It is one of the most popular self-clinging wall plants, capable of covering whole buildings with its relatively small leaves which colour brilliantly in autumn. A particularly good form is 'Lowei'.

Passiflora caerulea

Deciduous, tendril climber. This is the Blue Passion Flower remarkable for the broad circle of blue-purple filaments in the otherwise white flower. There is an all-white variety named 'Constance Elliot'. Both are rather tender but may survive for many years on sunny walls in milder parts of Britain. Even when cut back by frost it can make 6m (20ft) of growth the following summer.

Passiflora caerulea **sometimes produces yellow fruits.**

Phygelius capensis

Evergreen shrub. In the open this plant will sprawl but against a wall it can be trained to a height of about 6m (20ft). The tubular flowers are scarlet and hang on curving stems in loose clusters from July to September. It is a little tender but usually survives against a sunny wall.

Polygonum baldschuanicum

Deciduous twiner. Popularly known as the Russian Vine, this is an extremely vigorous plant with huge clusters of small, creamy or pink-tinged flowers in September–October. Ideal for covering unsightly buildings or running high into trees.

Pyracantha atalantioides

Evergreen shrub. One of the strongest growing Firethorns, capable of clothing a high wall with little support. Its sprays of small, white flowers in early summer are followed by small but abundant scarlet fruits which usually remain for a long time.

Pyracantha 'Mohave'

Evergreen shrub. A moderately vigorous, hybrid Firethorn with quite large, orange berries.

Pyracantha rogersiana

Evergreen shrub. A relatively small-leaved species with fine sprays of white flowers in June followed by berries which are orange-red in variety 'Aurantiaca' and bright yellow in 'Flava'.

Pyracantha 'Orange Glow'

Evergreen shrub. Strong growing hybrid with spiny branches and quite large, orange-red berries.

Phygelius capensis

Polygonum baldschuanicum

Pyracantha rogersiana 'Flava'

Rosa 'Albertine', a *wichuraiana* rambler

Rosa 'Albéric Barbier'
Semi-evergreen rambler. This very vigorous rose has dark green, glossy leaves that, in a mild winter, will be almost completely retained. The double flowers are creamy-white and abundantly produced in June.

Rosa 'Albertine'
Deciduous rambler. Quite large, sweetly-scented, coppery-pink flowers in June. Strong, very thorny growth.

Rosa 'American Pillar'
Deciduous rambler, less lax than most. The very strong stems are quite stout and very thorny. Single, rose and white flowers are carried in large clusters in July.

Rosa 'Compassion'
Deciduous climber. Well shaped, apricot-pink flowers all summer. Moderate growth.

Rosa 'Danse du Feu'
Deciduous climber. Clusters of medium size, orange-red flowers all summer. Moderate growth.

Rosa 'Dublin Bay'
Deciduous climber. Clusters of medium size, crimson flowers all summer. Moderate growth.

Rosa 'Golden Showers'
Deciduous climber. Clusters of quite large, bright yellow flowers in June-July with a few more later in the summer. Moderate growth.

Rosa 'Pink Perpetue'

Rosa 'Handel'
Deciduous climber. Shapely, pink and white flowers of medium size, all summer. Grows to about 4m (13ft).

Rosa 'Kiftsgate'
Deciduous rambler. Huge clusters of single, creamy-white, richly-scented flowers in June–July. Once established, will reach 9m (30ft) and can ascend tall trees. Thorny.

Rosa 'Madame Alfred Carrière'
Deciduous climber. Small clusters of quite large, double flowers, cream in bud but white when fully open. They are sweetly scented and mainly produced in June–July but a few more usually come later. It has few thorns and is sufficiently vigorous to cover a house wall.

**Rosa
'Madame Grégoire Staechelin'**
Deciduous climber. Large, fully double, richly-scented flowers, carmine in bud, rose pink when open. Flow-

ers in June–July only but there are large hips to follow, green becoming reddish-brown. Vigorous and fine for a house wall.

Rosa 'Maigold'
Deciduous climber. Medium size, semi-double, apricot-yellow flowers, mainly in June–July but a few to follow. Good, glossy green foliage. Moderately vigorous; very thorny.

Rosa 'Mermaid'
Deciduous climber. Large, single, light yellow flowers all summer. Glossy, dark green leaves and strong growth with big thorns but this rose is apt to die back if hard pruned. Only thin lightly and cut out dead or diseased stems. This variety does well trained on a partially shaded wall, if protected from hard frosts.

Rosa 'New Dawn'
Deciduous rambler. Clusters of medium size, double, pale pink flowers, borne throughout the summer months. Strong growth to 4m (13ft) or even more.

Rosa 'Maigold'

44

Rosa 'Pink Perpetue'

Deciduous climber. Clusters of medium size, rose-pink flowers all summer. Will reach 4m (13ft).

Rosa 'Schoolgirl'

Deciduous climber. Fairly large, apricot flowers all summer. Moderate vigour.

Rosa 'Seagull'

Deciduous rambler. Large clusters of small single, white flowers in June. Moderate vigour; will grow to about 4m (13ft).

Rosa 'Veilchenblau'

Deciduous rambler. Clusters of small, double, violet-purple flowers, fading to lilac in July. Will reach about 3.5m (12ft). Very few thorns.

Rosa 'Zéphirine Drouhin'

Deciduous climber. Large, fully double, rose-pink, scented flowers all summer. Thornless stems of moderate vigour to about 3m (10ft).

Rubus laciniatus

Deciduous bramble. This is popularly known as the Cut-leaved or Fern-leaved Blackberry, both of which give a good idea of its appearance. It grows just like an ordinary blackberry and produces good crops of well-flavoured berries but its leaves are finely divided and distinctly ornamental. It will reach 3m (10ft), has no natural means of support other than its thorns and, in gardens, must be tied to wires, posts or other supports.

Rubus phoenicolasius

Deciduous bramble. A relative of the blackberry, known as the Japanese Wineberry. The long stems are densely covered with purple bristles and the red fruits are much like loganberries but inferior in flavour. Stems need to be tied to supports.

Rubus phoenicolasius

45

Schizophragma integrifolium

Schizophragma integrifolium

Deciduous, self-clinging climber. This is a relative of the climbing hydrangea and climbs in the same way, by aerial roots. It differs in the formation of the flat flower clusters which have fewer but larger creamy-white bracts. The clusters can be as much as 30cm (1ft) in diameter and are very handsome in July–August. The plant can reach 9m (30ft).

Solanum crispum

Semi-evergreen sprawler. Left to its own devices this plant will make a big, sprawling bush or push its way up through stronger shrubs. It is more effective if trained against a sunny wall or screen or over a pergola where its large clusters of flowers will be well displayed. They are purplish-blue with a cone of yellow stamens in the centre like those of a potato to which it is related. Its popular name is Potato Vine. It flowers from June to September. 'Glasnevin' is a good, free-flowering variety.

Tropaeolum speciosum

Herbaceous twiner. This striking plant has rather fleshy roots and long, slender stems with small, deeply-lobed leaves and small but very numerous, scarlet, nasturtium-like flowers. It is popularly known as the Flame Flower and it likes to scramble up through other plants. In Scotland and the north of England where it grows particularly well, it can often be seen covering yew hedges with trails of brilliant scarlet flowers from July onwards. Plants should be obtained in pots, preferably in spring, and be planted without root breakage in fairly rich, rather moist soil.

Solanum crispum 'Glasnevin'

Trachelospermum jasminoides

Evergreen twiner. The glossy dark green leaves make good cover for a wall and the small but abundant white flowers in July–August fill the air with sweet jasmine perfume. There is a variety named 'Variegatum' with cream variegated leaves. Plants are a little tender but in most places safe on a south-facing wall.

Vitis 'Brant'

Deciduous, tendril climber. A handsome hybrid vine with leaves that become bronzy-red in the autumn except for the veins which remain green. The juice of the small, black fruits is pleasant to drink or can be used to make wine.

Vitis coignetiae

Deciduous, tendril climber. One of the most vigorous of all vines, capable of reaching the top of a tall tree. The leaves are also very large, up to 30cm (1ft) across and more or less round. They colour vividly in the autumn.

Vitis vinifera 'Purpurea'

Deciduous, tendril climber. A decorative variety of the common grape vine with claret-red leaves, turning to a spectacular deep purple.

Vitis vinifera 'Brant'

Wisteria sinensis

Wisteria floribunda

Deciduous twiner. A species of moderate vigour, excellent for covering arbours, pergolas and so on. Typically the long, scented flower trails in May-June are violet-blue but there are white, pink and purple varieties.

Wisteria sinensis

Deciduous twiner. This is the strongest growing kind, capable of ascending to the tops of tall trees. It is often propagated by seeds but seedlings tend to be variable in quality so it is wise to buy either from a reliable nurseryman or while the plants are in flower. Colour can be anything from a rather pale greyish-blue to clear lilac-blue and there is a white variety named 'Alba'. There are also numerous garden varieties, mainly of Japanese origin, which are probably hybrids with *W. floribunda* and have variously coloured flowers: white, light blue, dark blue and pink.

INDEX AND ACKNOWLEDGEMENTS

Picture credits

Pat Brindley: 11(b),13(b),14(l),15(t,b),16(r),17(b),22(t),32(t), 34(t,b),35(t),36(t),37(r),38(r),39(t,b),42(br),43,44(t,b),46(b).
Lyn and Derek Gould: 17(t).
Arthur Hellyer: 12,16(l),46(t).
ICI: 27(bl, br).
Harry Smith Horticultural Photographic Collection: 4/5,6,7(t,b), 9,10,11(t),13(t),14(r),18,20,23(t,b),24,25(t),26,28/9,30,31(t,b), 32(b),33(l,r),35(b),36(b),37(l),38(l),40(t,b),41,42(t,bl),45,47(t,b).
Michael Warren: 1,22(b),27(t).

Artwork by Simon Roulstone